STALIN
AND THE
KIROV MURDER

By the Same Author

STALIN
AND THE
KIROV MURDER

Robert Conquest

OXFORD UNIVERSITY PRESS
New York   Oxford

OXFORD UNIVERSITY PRESS

Oxford   New York   Toronto
Delhi   Bombay   Calcutta   Madras   Karachi
Petaling Jaya   Singapore   Hong Kong   Tokyo
Nairobi   Dar es Salaam   Cape Town
Melbourne   Auckland

and associated companies in
Berlin   Ibadan

Library of Congress Cataloging-in-Publication Data
Conquest, Robert.
Stalin and the Kirov murder / Robert Conquest.
p.   cm.   Bibliography: p.   Includes index.
1. Kirov, Sergei Mironovich, 1886–1934—Assassination.   2. Stalin,
Joseph, 1879–1953.   3. Terrorism—Soviet Union.   4. Soviet Union—
Politics and government—1917–1936.   I. Title.
DK254.K52C66   1989   947.084'2'0924—dc 19
88–11994   CIP
ISBN 0-19-505579-9
ISBN 0-19-506337-6 (pbk.)

2 4 6 8 10 9 7 5 3 1

Printed in the United States of America

For Daisy and Thomas

Preface

By the time this book comes out it may be that Soviet official condemnation of Stalin for the murder of Kirov will have appeared. It seems nearly to have done so thirty years ago. And in recent months it has been very strongly implied, or even said directly in odd publications—though it is true that the Stalinist allegation of "opposition" responsibility was still to be found as late as the winter of 1987–1988.

Stalin's guilt is indeed scarcely in doubt, though this final verification will be welcome. But it is unlikely that the full story of the complex plot which led to the murder will be fully described at any early date: still less that the extraordinary details of Stalin's use of it against his rivals and colleagues will be fully presented. Meanwhile, the time is clearly ripe for a complete examination of all the evidence, and an account of the way truths came out, gradually and piecemeal, first in the West, and later in the USSR.

In fact, we can, with all the old and new evidence, make a full examination of one of the most astonishing and most significant episodes of the century, which is at the same time a story of a long effort of detection faced with obfuscation.

One point that emerges is how accurate Soviet samizdat accounts, dating back up to twenty years, have turned out to be. And, indeed, how generally sound (if not accurate in every detail) some second-hand, usually defector, sources of an even earlier period have proved. Both types of evidence have often been subjected in the West not to careful critical handling, but to dogmatic rejection. Thus in addition to all that the case can teach us about the Stalin era, and about political assassination and falsification, it is also a lesson on the mature treatment of history and historical evidence.

My thanks are due in particular to the John Olin Program for the Study of the Soviet Union and Eastern Europe at the Hoover Institution; to Helena Stone and Delano DuGarm for invaluable research and other help; to Amy Desai, for her usual accuracy and diligence in preparing the manuscript; to the resources of the Hoover Library and Archives which have, as ever, served me well; and, especially, to my wife.

R. C.

Stanford, California
July 1988

Contents

Contents

Leading Characters

Agranov, Yakov (Yan) Saulovich — Deputy, People's Commissar, NKVD. Shot c. 1937.

Bakayev, Ivan Petrovich — Zinovievite; former Head, Leningrad GPU. Shot 1936.

Bal'tsevich, M. S. — Leningrad NKVD, probably Operative Department. Shot c. 1937.

Borisov [fnu] — Head of Kirov's bodyguard. Murdered 1934.

Bukharin, Nikolai Ivanovich — Former member, Politburo. Shot 1938.

Chudov, Mikhail Semenovich — Second Secretary, Leningrad. Shot 1937.

Draule, Milda — Nikolayev's wife. Believed shot 1934 or 1935.

Evdokimov, Grigori Eremeevich — Former Secretary, Central Committee (CC). Shot 1936.

Fomin, Fedor Timofeevich — Deputy Head, Leningrad NKVD. Imprisoned 1935; survived.

Kaganovich, Lazar Moiseevich — Politburo member. Survived.

Kamenev, Lev Borisovich — Former member, Politburo. Shot 1936.

Khrushchev, Nikita Sergeevich — Later First Secretary, CC, Communist Party of the Soviet Union (CPSU). Died 1971.

Kirov, Sergei Mironovich — Leningrad First Secretary; Secretary, CC. Murdered 1934.

Kodatsky, Ivan Fedorovich — Chairman, Leningrad City Executive Committee. Shot 1937.

Kosarev, Alexandr Vasilevich — General Secretary, Komsomol. Shot 1939.

Kotolynov, Ivan Ivanovich — Leningrad Communist; ex-Zinovievite. Shot 1934.

Kuznetsov, Aleksei Aleksandrovich — Later First Secretary, Leningrad. Shot 1950.

Levin, Vladimir Solomonovich — Leningrad Communist; ex-Zinovievite. Shot 1934.

Lyushkov, Genrikh Samoilovich — Deputy Head, Secret Political Department, NKVD. Defected to Japan 1938; died 1945.

Medved, Filip Demyanovich — Head, Leningrad NKVD. Shot c. 1937 (?).

Mikoyan, Anastas Ivanovich — Candidate member, later full member of the Politburo. Died 1978.

Nikolayev, Leonid Vasilevich — Kirov's murderer. Shot 1934.

Ordzhonikidze, Grigori (Sergo) Konstantinovich — Member, Politburo. Suicide or murdered 1937.

Poskrebyshev, Alexandr Nikolaevich — Stalin's secretary. Died 1966(?).

Pozern, Boris Pavlovich — Secretary, Leningrad City Committee. Shot 1939.

Rumyantsev, Vladimir Vasilevich — Leningrad Communist; ex-Zinovievite. Shot 1934.

Rykov, Aleksei Ivanovich — Former member, Politburo, Chairman, Council of People's Commissars. Shot 1938.

Shaposhnikova, Lyudmila — Chudov's wife; Secretary, Leningrad Trade Unions. Shot c. 1938.

Shatsky, Nikolai Nikolaevich — Leningrad engineer. Shot 1934.

Stalin, Josif Vissarionovich — General Secretary, CC; later Prime Minister. Died 1953.

Struppe, Petr I. — Chairman, Leningrad Provincial Executive Committee. Shot 1937.

Trotsky, Lev Davidovich — Former member, Politburo. Murdered 1940.

Ugarov, Aleksandr Ivanovich — Secretary, Leningrad City Committee. Shot 1939.

Ulrikh, Vasil Vasilevich — Chairman, Military Collegium of the Supreme Court. Died 1950.

Volovich, A. I. — Deputy Head, Operative Department, NKVD. Shot c. 1937.

Voroshilov, Kliment Efremovich	Member, Politburo. Died 1969.
Vyshinsky, Andrei Yanuarevich	Deputy Prosecutor-General; later Prosecutor-General, USSR. Died 1954.
Yagoda, Genrikh Grigorevich	People's Commissar, NKVD. Shot 1938.
Yenukidze, Avel Safronovich	Secretary, Central Executive Committee. Shot 1937.
Yezhov, Nikolai Ivanovich	Head, Cadres Department, CC; later Secretary, CC and People's Commissar, NKVD. Shot 1940.
Zakovsky, Leonid Mikhailovich	Head, Leningrad NKVD (from December 1934). Shot 1939.
Zaporozhets, Ivan V.	Deputy Head, Leningrad NKVD. Shot c. 1938.
Zhdanov, Andrei Aleksandrovich	First Secretary, Leningrad (from December 1934). Died 1948.
Zinoviev, Grigori Evseevich	Former member, Politburo. Shot 1936.

STALIN
AND THE
KIROV MURDER

Introduction

This century has seen horrible crimes on a mass scale, culminating in the Jewish Holocaust. No comparison with these can be sustained. But as an individual murder, there is, for various reasons, none to match the Kirov case.

Single events—even accidental ones—have often turned the path of history. The assassination of the Archduke Franz Ferdinand, just over twenty years previously, brought on a perhaps otherwise avoidable Great War. At any rate, that is the only individual crime (or dual crime, since the Archduke's morganatic wife was also killed) with which the Kirov murder can remotely be compared. But even the assassination of the Archduke had no further intrinsic result beyond the crisis leading to war. There was no mystery about the responsibility. No long-lasting policies were based on any theoretical view of it.

The Kirov murder, however, was made the central justification for the whole theory of Stalinism and the necessity for endless terror. For many years the responsibility was laid on those ex-oppositionist Communists whom Stalin had defeated but who had become reconciled with the Party. At one of their many trials for the murder, Andrei Vyshinsky was able to quote Stalin's formulation of 1933, about the inevitability of the "resistance of the last remnants of the dying classes" both increasing and including a "re-

vival of the activities of the fragments of counterrevolutionary opposition elements from among the Trotskyites and the Right de-
viationists." As Vyshinsky pointed out, "this trial has fully and
distinctly proved the great wisdom of this forecast."

It had previously been thought that the destruction of all hostile classes and the introduction of socialism would mean the dying down of the class struggle—and such was the view taken by
Kirov and others. Stalin was propounding a new theoretical idea:
that the crushing of the class enemy meant the intensification of a
now desperate resistance. An ideological basis was thus provided
for a new and fierce struggle, in which the state would be facing
fanatical representatives of the class enemy. And, since no other
political force remained to represent the defeated classes, oppositionist (or ex-oppositionist) Communists were inevitably given the
task. Opposition to the Party line led inevitably to degeneration
into a bourgeois position.

The other element was 'capitalist encirclement'. While the rest
of the world remained unsocialist or antisocialist, bourgeois remnants within the USSR who had lost any local support would rely
on foreign states. Oppositionist Communists would be driven by
the logic of their position to come to terms with bourgeois, and
especially fascist, governments.

The Kirov murder demonstrated that the enemy was now driven
to extreme courses. If the enemy was merely an aggrieved eccen-
tric assassin, this would not amount to much. As a member of a
politically oriented group, linked to the whole underworld of dis-
gruntled and defeated Party faction, he became a historical phenomenon, the emblem of a new phase of terror and counterterror.

For this was not merely a theoretical matter. The murder is certainly unique in the number who perished as a result of it. In the
years which followed—and especially in 1937–1938—first thou-
sands, then literally millions of people were accused of membership of various branches of a vast conspiracy whose main and major
crime was the Kirov assassination. As a prominent victim says,
"the year 1937 really began on the 1st December 1934"—the
date of Kirov's death.

It was, then, the key moment which determined the development of the Soviet system, and so the future of the world.

George Orwell's dictum, that the Communists "pretended, perhaps they even believed, that they had seized power unwillingly and for a limited time, and that just round the corner there lay a paradise where human beings would be free and equal," is a valuable insight into the way people think and justify themselves to themselves. But within that formulation one may envisage those in whose original motives the humanistic element, even though overridden in practice by the power motive, was at least stronger than with others. For Bukharin, perhaps for Kirov, the indefinite postponement of *all* the justifications of what they had done, rode less well than with Stalin, or such henchmen of his as Kaganovich. If an assassin, or an accident, had instead carried off Stalin in 1934, it seems certain that Kirov and his associates would have prevailed. And at the very least the Soviet Union would have developed differently in major respects.

The murder is also probably unique in the layers of misdirection by which suspicion and attention were diverted; in the variety of suspects; in the series of different explanations put forward, supported by false confessions—all in all more than enough to satisfy any connoisseur of crime fiction.

The assessment of historical evidence is a refractory task. But it does not differ essentially from some of the judgments we all have to make in our ordinary lives. If the Stalin period is a particularly obscure area, it is only because so much official falsification took place and because unofficial sources are difficult to assess.

However, the official accounts contain much of significance amidst the falsification. The unofficial accounts are of varying credibility, and they, too, need careful handling. Any criminal lawyer, indeed any constant reader of novels of detection, knows that evidence may come from all sorts of witnesses; that even first-hand testimony, let alone second-hand, may be confused, exaggerated, distorted by opinion or by misunderstanding, and yet contain truths which may valuably supplement and clarify other evidence. Moreover, two accounts may differ in detail, and yet clearly tell the same story, complementing and confirming each other as to the main event. We shall be treading a complex, and fascinating, path.

It is only now—more than fifty years later—that the country in which the murder took place is beginning to bring out the whole truth of the matter. Meanwhile, evidence of the most varied sort has been available for many years, and there is little doubt that the material assembled in this book gives, if perhaps not yet as to certain details, a sound account of what happened.

CHAPTER I

The Murder

On 2 December 1934, *Pravda* announced that "on 1 December, at 16:30, in the city of Leningrad in the building of the Leningrad Soviet (former Smolny), at the hands of a murderer, a concealed enemy of the working class, died Secretary of the Central and Leningrad Committees of the All-Union Communist Party (Bolshevik) and member of the Presidium of the Central Executive Committee of the USSR, Comrade Sergei Mironovich Kirov. The gunman has been arrested. His identity is being established."

The Smolny, a handsome structure with a classical front of pillars and pediment, set in its own park facing eastward up the Neva, was where Kirov had his offices. Seventeen years earlier the former aristocratic girls' school had been the headquarters from which Lenin directed the seizure of power. Since the transfer of the capital to Moscow, it had been the center from which not only Leningrad city and province, but the whole Soviet Northwest, was controlled. Kirov's offices and those of other local leaders were on the third floor (i.e., the British second floor).

Kirov had returned on 29 November from a plenary session of the Central Committee of the Communist Party in Moscow. The other Leningrad members of that Committee had accompanied him: in particular his number two, and most trusted colleague, the "shockheaded" Mikhail Chudov, Second Secretary of the Leningrad Provincial Committee of the Party; and his other "closest collaborators,"[1] as an official biography puts it, the "elegant" I. F. Kodatsky, head of the city's government as Chairman of its Executive Committee; P. A. Alekseyev, Chairman of the Leningrad Trade Unions; A. I. Ugarov, Secretary of the City Committee; P. I. Struppe, Chairman of the Provincial Executive Committee; and B. P. Pozern and P. I. Smorodin, Secretaries of the City Committee, Kirov, Chudov, Kodatsky, and Alekseyev were full members, and the others candidate members, of the Central Committee.

They had already reported to the Leningrad Committees, and on the evening of 1 December the whole of the active membership—the aktiv—of the city's party were to assemble for a more public report at the Tavride Palace. Soon after 4 P.M. Kirov arrived at the Smolny to confer with Chudov and others on the text of the report. It was already dark and there was snow on the ground.[2]

According to one official Soviet biography "his personal guard" had accompanied him in his car but did not follow him upstairs into the Smolny.[3] This man, a veteran called Borisov, is described as devoted to Kirov. He had been detained by men of the People's Commissariat of Internal Affairs (NKVD), and is next heard of at Leningrad NKVD headquarters.[4] He had two days to live.

Kirov went up to his office without him, perhaps not noticing that the usual guards on each floor were also absent.

All accounts agree that the assassin had entered the Smolny without difficulty, and gone up to the third floor.[5] He had earlier worked there, and had a good knowledge of the building.[6] He seems to have hidden in a lavatory, from which he watched the arrival of Kirov's car.[7]

Kirov first conferred briefly with Chudov and others. There is some divergence even in official accounts, and more in others, about which room this meeting took place in, but this is of no great significance. In any case, it seems that he left Chudov's office, or more probably his own reception room,[8] and walked along the corridor to his "working office."[9] To reach it, he had to make a left turn, which allowed the assassin, emerging from his retreat, to shoot him in the back of the neck.[10]

The next divergence in the accounts is of more significance. In most, only one shot is mentioned or assumed, but some speak of two shots,[11] the second fired by the assassin in a suicide attempt, but missing him and hitting the ceiling. One report has a different explanation for this second shot (see pp. 134–35).

In any case, the assassin fainted and fell beside his victim. Chudov and the others hurried out into the corridor. Kirov was carried bleeding and unconscious into his office and, when the doctors came, was given adrenalin, ether, camphor, and caffeine, but he soon died.[12] The autopsy gives in great detail the path of the bullet and its effects. It was also established that a Nagan revolver was used, and that this was what was found near the assassin.[13] Meanwhile, NKVD men arrested the unconscious killer, and Chudov telephoned the news to Moscow.

The murder was not done on impulse. The assassin had been preparing his act since the summer. But after various setbacks, his final written plan of the campaign is dated 1 November 1934, in the interrogation records.[14]

It will be seen that there were already some suspicious circumstances. The mere fact of an assassin seeking to kill Kirov is easily enough understood (though his precise motives remained to be established). The question was, how did he get the opportunity? Why were the Smolny guards absent? Where was Kirov's own bodyguard?

Or, to put it another way, who gave him his chance, and why?

CHAPTER II

The Assassin

On 3 December it was announced that preliminary investigation had established that the assassin was Leonid Vasilevich Nikolayev, born 1904, a former worker in the Leningrad Workers' and Peasants' Inspection (RKI), and that the investigation was continuing.[1]

Nikolayev, aged thirty, is said (like Stalin) to have had a drunken father who beat him.[2] He had a malformed leg.[3] He is also reported as subject to some kind of fit.[4] His physical constitution was, in general, weak. His psychological or nervous makeup was even more unfortunate.

He had joined the Communist Party in 1920, at the age of sixteen,[5] and took part in the city squads engaged in the mass seizure of grain from the peasantry, which was a mark of the period.[6]

When things settled down, he got a job in a factory, but the work was hard for him physically, and at the same time he felt himself capable of and entitled to an official post. He finally got such a position, in the RKI.[7] He seems to have been found inadequate and was demoted to a lesser post, though still an administrative one. However, early in 1934 the local Party mobilized members for tractor stations, railway work, and so on, and Nikolayev was ordered to report for one of these. He refused on health grounds and in March was expelled from the Party for breach of its discipline. However, two months later he was reinstated, having apparently appealed to Moscow,[8] and having made "a declaration of repentance."[9]

He was, however, able to avoid being sent to labor, this time successfully pleading health problems. But he was not given an official post, and seems to have had no work for the rest of the year. He had by this time developed a single-minded hatred of the bureaucracy, which he blamed for failing to give him his due and ignoring his problems.

He began to see himself as an assassin on the historic scale. One report has him saying at an early interrogation "in times to come my name will be coupled with those of Zhelyabov and Balmashev," the great assassins of the Russian past.[10] A senior interrogator in the case confirms that he studied the historic terrorists, like Charlotte Corday, and modeled himself on them.[11]

Many of the revolutionary generation had been in some sense misfits; at any rate, they had found it hard to adjust to the stricter order of the Stalin period.

A foreign Communist who had lived in Leningrad in the early thirties saw Kirov and his subordinates as establishmentarian administrators, adding that "in the office of Kirov, governor of Leningrad in 1929, one felt that the revolution had already been tamed and canalised. I was to interpret Nikolayev's revolver-shot as an act arising from the despair of the 1917–1924 generation, disappointed with the results of the revolution and the Five Year Plan, without the strength to begin all over again."[12]

Nikolayev was married to a woman named Milda Draule, and had two children. His father was dead, but his mother, Maria T. Nikolayeva, an Old Believer who worked in a tram depot, was still alive, having just received an award for thirty years service. He also had a brother, Petr; a sister, Katerina Rogacheva; a half-sister, Anna Pantyukhina; a sister-in-law, Petr's wife A. A. Nikolayeva-Maximova—all of whom were to suffer through the case.[13]

His wife was a Latvian, and on friendly terms with the wife of the Latvian Consul, George Bissenieks (a connection later worked into the accusation).[14] She had a secretarial job at Party headquarters, and after the assassination a story was put about that she was having an affair with Kirov and that Nikolayev had killed him out of jealousy.[15] There seems no doubt that this rumor, which gained wide credence in Party and diplomatic circles, is untrue; and though described as 'beautiful' for the purposes of the story, the only first-hand description we have of her, for what it is worth, describes her as rather ugly.[16] A Soviet writer suggests that one of the motives of the police-sponsored rumor was to denigrate Kirov.[17]

There is no genuine evidence that Nikolayev had political motives in a broader sense. In particular, he had never been in trouble with the Party because of association with the Zinoviev "opposition," which had controlled Leningrad until 1926, nor of links with local former members of that opposition (long since readmitted to the Party and in 1934 largely reconciled to it and particularly to Kirov).[18] One report has it, in fact, that Nikolayev had been particularly strong against the Zinovievites during the struggles of the 1920s when Zinoviev and his 'Left' faction had made their bid for power against Stalin and his then allies, the 'Right' led by Bukharin.[19]

Nikolayev's briefcase, searched on his arrest, contained a diary, and "statements addressed to various institutions." In these he gave his motives as "a personal act of desperation and dissatisfaction arising out of his straitened material circumstances and as a protest against the unjust attitude of certain members of the government towards a live person."[20]

G. Lyushkov, deputy head of the NKVD Secret Political Department, one of the leading interrogators in the case, tells us:

> Nikolayev lacked balance, he had many problems. In short, he was dissatisfied with life. He was convinced that he was capable of any work. He also felt he was hard to understand. He was always discontented, and did not get on with people easily. . . . All his efforts led to his losing his official positions. This attitude on the part of society drove him to the belief that the problem was not in his personal faults, but in the institutions. This discontent in turn drove him into his scheme to assassinate some important figure in the Party. Through this act he wished to protest against the bureaucratism and heartlessness of the Party organs.[21]

The assassin was indeed described in *Pravda* of 3 December 1934 as "an enemy of the working class" by the Central Committee, as "an enemy of Soviet power" by the Central Executive Committee, and as an "enemy of the workers and peasants" by the Council of Peoples' Commissars. But the attribution of political, oppositionist motives to him evidently distorts his real feelings. He did indeed want to strike a blow against bureaucracy, but this was because of its supposed persecution of himself. This does not mean that he had not to some degree generalized his hostility into a political animus in his own mind. However, his would not be the first assassination carried out by a "disappointed office-seeker"—as the assassin of President Garfield in 1881 is described.

Nikolayev seems to have spoken freely to some of his acquaintance about his hatred of the "bureaucracy," and with one (unidentified) friend he had, as we shall see, not only discussed the whole project but gone out with him to practice revolver shooting.[22] (In the official account, Nikolayev later confessed to having "tried out" over the months August–November 1934, the "Nagan revolver he possessed."[23])

It will be asked how the Leningrad security branch of the NKVD had failed to learn of all this. The answer, of course, is that they were fully informed. And Nikolayev, as we shall also see, had already twice been arrested with a revolver in Kirov's vicinity but both times released on orders from above. The second time was apparently while trying to enter the Smolny itself.[24]

Nikolayev's personal motivations soon ceased to be the main point. The official version came to be first that he was, in fact, part of a widespread conspiracy; and later that the NKVD had played a part in that conspiracy and had made sure that Nikolayev had access to his victim.

CHAPTER III

Kirov the Bolshevik

If in writing of Nikolayev we are faced with a certain lack of data, with Kirov the problem is quite different. About him a great deal has been written, but it is almost entirely in terms of conventional adulation. Even so, we can form a reasonably clear picture of the dead leader.

Sergei Mironovich Kostrikov, his original name, was born in 1886 in Urzhum, a small town in the Vyatka (now Kirov) Province in northern Russia, into a petty bourgeois family.

He lost his parents at an early age. His father 'raged and drank' and abandoned his family. His mother died soon after and he was brought up in part by his grandmother, in part in a local orphanage. From 1901 to 1904 he went to a vocational school in Kazan, the nearest city, where he trained as a mechanic. He met radical students from the local university and was soon printing leaflets for them. He went on to the Siberian city of Tomsk, where he joined the Social Democratic Party. He became noted, at the age of nineteen, for party activity.[1]

During a liberal 'banquet', part of the campaign for a constitution, he held the guests up at gunpoint to listen to local Social Democrats. He became involved with the party's armed groups, servicing and distributing guns.[2] And in 1905 he was elected to the party committee in Tomsk. He helped organize the railway strikes that greatly affected the outcome of the 1905 revolution and the Tsar's grant of a constitution—which, however, largely disarmed the revolutionary wave.

In 1906 he was arrested, being released in 1909. He settled in Vladikavkaz to the far south, the key to the Caucasus, where he got a job with the local liberal newspaper *Terek,* took the name Kirov, and married Maria Markus. Her sister, a Bolshevik, lived in St. Petersburg, and was always thought of as his 'party godmother'.[3]

In 1911 he was arrested again, though released for lack of evidence. Over the next few years he was prominent in illegal printing, and strike work, and got to know Lenin's directives.[4]

Lenin's men had long been regarded as particularly authoritarian and extreme even among the revolutionary sects. Rosa Luxemburg had spoken of their despotic tendency and also of their "Tatar–Mongolian savagery." They were, in effect, a small millenarian sect, with a set of unquestioned dogmas about the attainment of the perfect society through class warfare. It was thus from an ambience of narrow and extreme doctrine that Kirov accepted his ideas and principles.

It was not until 1912 that the Bolsheviks, hitherto one of a number of polemical factions within the Russian Social Democrats, became a separate party. At this time, Trotsky tells us, the membership of all Social Democrats together was under 10,000; the Bolsheviks must have been considerably fewer. It was a very small pool from which to provide the leadership of a large country.

Moreover, the Menshevik Sukhanov, whose memoirs of the revolution Lenin much admired, noted an extraordinary lack of talent among the Bolsheviks. In the seizure of power, it is remarkable how many of the decisive figures were to be from the 'Mezhrayontsi'—Trotsky's dissident Mensheviks whose dislike of Lenin's bureaucratic centralism was overridden by his presenting the only radical program for instant revolution.

The Trotskyites and others were a small handful, and the USSR was to be ruled thenceforward, and until the mid-1930s, largely by those who had been members of a party which five years before the Revolution had been a small sect with a few thousand followers. And one, moreover, in which centralism and bureaucracy had tended to discourage recruits of initiative and independent-mindedness. Indeed, it was Lenin's old favorites Zinoviev, Kamenev, and Rykov who proved timid in the seizure of power. Lenin had to forgive these three and others simply because there was no one else to turn to. In the same way, the 'Left' Communists of 1918, who opposed the Brest Litovsk Treaty—Bukharin and the others—were immediately welcomed back when the particular quarrel was over.

In this context, or ambience, the crises of the Revolution, and even more of the Civil War, threw up a comparatively small selection of men with the capacity for instant, ruthless decision and the ability to master dangerous and desperate situations. Kirov was one of them.

Even when the Bolsheviks seized power, their membership was only a few hundred thousand. Lenin remarked that if a few hundred thousand nobles and capitalists could rule Russia, so could that number of Communists, though he later asserted that the latter's 'culture' was incomparably lower.

This smallish membership, and later recruits, formed the rank and file in the critical years after the revolution. The Party continued to be run, almost exclusively, by the old cadres. And, as Lenin was to write, Party policy was "determined at present not by its rank and file, but by the immense and undivided authority of the tiny section which might be called the Party's Old Guard."[5]

When the February Revolution came, Kirov and a few colleagues (in particular M. Orakhelashvili and N. Gikalo) worked to forward party aims in Vladikavkaz, though the majority in the local Soviet were non-Bolshevik. He was one of the delegates to the All-Russian Congress of Soviets in October, when Lenin seized power.

From now on the Bolsheviks, driven from the Caucasus, faced a desperate and complex struggle. Kirov was given the key post of leader of the Military Revolutionary Committee in Astrakhan, near the mouth of the Volga, from which the penetration of the Caucasus had to be organized.

There, as a good Bolshevik, he suppressed a workers' rising.[6] (His comrades included Bagirov, the sponsor and colleague of Beria who later figures as one of the carefully selected infiltra-

tors of independent Georgia, under Kirov's aegis).[7] Important
Bolsheviks—Ordzhonikidze, Kuibyshev, Mikoyan—were also sent
to this key city.[8] One of Kirov's most trusted later colleagues,
I. F. Kodatsky, had a post there.[9]

In February 1920, the Central Committee formed a Bureau for
restoring Soviet Government in the North Caucasus, with Ordzhonikidze as Chairman and Kirov as Vice-Chairman. By April
the Red Army had captured Baku. Kirov served on the four-
member Trans-Caucasian Bureau.[10] Its main task was simple and
brutal. Georgia had been an independent Social Democratic Republic for two years. In its elections the Bolsheviks had won only
a few thousand votes and not a single seat. In a treaty signed with
Georgia on 7 May 1920, Lenin's government "unreservedly rec-
ognizes the independence and sovereign rights of the Georgian
State and voluntarily renounces all sovereign rights"; it also "un-
dertakes to refrain from any kind of interference in the internal
affairs of Georgia." But Georgia was now geographically and stra-
tegically outflanked. Kirov was appointed Soviet ambassador. Lenin briefed him. On his arrival he started to organize the meager
Georgian Bolshevik Party. He hid its chief, M. Orakhelashvili, in
the Soviet embassy.[11] In fact, the embassy was no more than an
implement in the Communist plan to seize Georgia.

In September Kirov was sent to help in peace negotiations with
the Poles, but was back in the Caucasus when in February 1921
a spurious Bolshevik rising in Tbilisi appealed for Soviet help,
and got it in the form of a Red Army invasion. Democratic Georgia was crushed by main force.

The events in the area between Astrakhan and what was to be
the southern Soviet border, ranging over Vladikavkaz and Baku
and Tbilisi, had been complex and refractory. They had called,
especially in the earlier phases, for both careful calculation and
ruthless daring on the part of the local Bolshevik leaders, especially Kirov who, moreover, was an excellent orator, the party's
best after Trotsky. He had, more than any of the other leaders,
the physical appearance of a Russian from the 'people'. And this,
too, stood him in increasingly good stead.

From 1921 to 1926, on the final establishment of the Bolshevik order, Kirov was Secretary of the Azerbaijan Central Com-

mittee. He proved himself a decisive and careful administrator. A candidate member of the Central Committee in 1921, he became a full member in 1923.

In 1926 he became a candidate member of the Politburo. After Lenin's first stroke in 1922, and even more so after his death in 1924, factional fighting at the highest level had become intense and bitter. First Trotsky was isolated by a coalition of Zinoviev and Kamenev, Bukharin and Rykov, and Stalin. Then a "New Opposition" uniting Zinoviev and Kamenev with their former enemy Trotsky was defeated by Stalin, Bukharin, Rykov, and others.

Zinoviev controlled the Leningrad party, where he was Chairman of the Soviet, with his henchman G. E. Evdokimov as Secretary of the Party organization. As Trotsky sardonically remarked, this meant that the delegations supposedly representing the proletariats of Leningrad and Moscow respectively voted 'unanimously' for different factions: what, he asked, was the social explanation?

Victory over Zinoviev at the Party Congress of 18–23 December 1925 still left him entrenched in Leningrad, and the next concern of the victors was to break his grip. But Zinovievite control was not really total. In the districts, and even in the delegations, there were Leningraders who were ripe to support Moscow. Even in 1923 Komarov, Kodatsky, and others had been on the Leningrad delegation to the Party Congress—though as yet not ready to break with the Zinovievites.

In December 1925–January 1926, a massive operation was launched in the city. Members of the Central Committee—Andreev, Voroshilov, Kalinin, Mikoyan, Ordzhonikidze (almost half the Politburo), and others—went to Leningrad and by continuous pressure at every Party level got the Zinovievites voted out piecemeal until, on 13 February, a new Provincial Committee headed by Kirov as the new First Secretary was 'elected', with N. K. Antipov as his deputy (until 1928 when he was replaced by Chudov). Kirov now enters the center of Party politics.

After the defeat of the Zinoviev–Trotsky 'Left', it appeared that the victorious majority of Stalin with Bukharin and the 'Rightists' was united in a policy of a fairly gradual elimination of the market system and the petty-bourgeois classes—in effect the independent peasantry.

The Party had been forced to retreat in 1921, when peasant rebellion and the Kronstadt revolt had led Lenin to abandon the immediate imposition of socialism and allow the re-emergence of the market in what was known as the New Economic Policy (NEP). His faithful followers had regretfully accepted the necessity, and had rebuffed the 'Left' who had tried to insist on an advance while the Party and state were still exhausted. By 1928, the economy had largely restored itself by these measures. And the Party had used the interval to strengthen and consolidate its power. It had, as it were, got its second wind. Many veterans now began to reject instinctively a mere continuation of the NEP which had failed to come to grips with Bolshevism's essential aims. In particular, they began to reject an ostentatiously 'gradualist' approach to the problem of a peasant majority which was both theoretically and practically hostile to the achievement of socialism.

Over the years 1926–1929, Stalin had gradually moved to isolating the 'Rightists', and, equally gradually, to a crash program against the peasantry—the 'Second Revolution' of collectivization and 'dekulakization' which did, in fact, destroy all classes unassimilable to a centralizing state-controlled socialism.

At first Stalin only urged a careful resumption of the advance. Until 1929 he maintained that he was still operating the New Economic Policy, combining it with ever tougher moves against the 'kulaks'. His tactics were in fact to hustle the Party, month by month, into a commitment to ever more radical assaults in the agrarian field. Some party leaders, like Molotov and Kaganovich, were wholehearted supporters of the hardest possible line. Others, like Kirov, were completely devoted in principle to an eventual crushing of the free peasantry and destruction of the market as the Leninist version of Marxism prescribes, but not yet convinced that the time had come.

At the Central Committee plenum of July 1928, the Rightists had even counted on Leningrad support. But Kirov and the Leningraders disassociated themselves from the only Rightist in their delegation, Stetsky.[12] Nevertheless in the autumn of 1928 we are told that Stalin had up to a point "met with a setback in attempting to win the Leningrad people to his cause—Komarov and the others—the successors of Zinoviev."[13]

At any rate, many of Kirov's associates did not feel the extreme hostility to the Right that Stalin was now purveying: in particular, Komarov, in Zinoviev's post as Chairman of the Leningrad Soviet, and F. Ya Ugarov, head of its Trade Unions. These were indeed demoted or transferred in 1929–1930, but even Kirov, while eventually throwing his weight against the Right, never showed the animus of the true Stalinist. In earlier Party disputes, even quite fierce ones, members of the defeated faction had often been reintegrated into the Party without malice. And, the whole attitude of Kirov's Leningraders, even though their vote was cast against the Rightists, does seem to have tended at least slightly in the semi-neutral direction Komarov took.

Kirov had rejected the Secretariat's efforts to dictate Leningrad appointments in 1926. He does not seem to have joined in the assault on Bukharin until April 1929, when it was all over. He had expressed reservations about Stalin's industrial plans.[14] And in 1928 and 1929, as Stephen F. Cohen notes, there were two Moscow attacks on the Leningrad Party—one on the local newspaper (resulting in the removal of its editor P. Petrovsky, son of the Politburo member) and one on its Control Commission.[15]

Kirov thus seems, in fact, to have been one of those not at first convinced that the time was ripe for crash collectivization. They came round to that view only after a series of suppositious grain shortages, handled by forced requisition, had left the agricultural economy badly shaken and confrontation began to seem inevitable. As Cohen has pointed out, Stalin's control of the Party organization gave him many advantages, but was by no means adequate by itself to victory over the NEP-oriented Right. Above all, it did not determine the way in which the higher level of leadership saw the issues. Kirov, quite typically, agreed with Stalin's point of view not in a servile way but in principle, at least as against the opposition. Stalin, in fact, now appeared to a hard core of old militants as representing the Party as against the talkative theorists of Left and Right.

The Right's call for restraint and concession in the face of the final "grain crisis" of 1928–1929 created an "aura of retreat and pessimism" around them, which was unwelcome to the Party veterans.[16] As Kirov himself put it, "In a word, the Rights are for socialism, but without particular fuss, without struggle, without difficulties."[17] This was much in line with Stalin's insistence that the class struggle was "at the root" of the dispute between him and the Right.[18] On the Politburo, Molotov and Kaganovich were already Stalinists pure and simple. Stalin may, as Bukharin suggested, have had a blackmail hold over Kalinin and Voroshilov. But Kirov, Kuibyshev, Rudzutak, Petrovsky, and the others plainly followed their political instincts. When the Party was finally committed to the collectivization struggle, they rallied to the attack. So generals may have reservations about a certain strategy yet, when it is decided on, do all they can to make it succeed.

In fact, the dangerous and vastly destructive campaign of collectivization, including the deportation of millions of so-called kulaks, had its attractions for the veterans, to whom it recalled the heroic days of 1917–1921. And when a really dangerous situation developed, the mood of desperate struggle gripped them. Even those who admitted that Bukharin's arguments were "mathematically correct" urged that this was irrelevant, for the same had applied to the Civil War, which Bolshevik will-power had nevertheless won.[19]

Over the harsh years 1930–1933 Kirov threw himself into the fight, led by Stalin, to crush the last class enemy, and bring in socialism. He was the very model of the hard-line old Bolshevik who rallied to the struggle for that final victory.

CHAPTER IV

Kirov and Stalin 1932-1934

Thus in the critical years 1929–1933 Kirov was a wholehearted supporter of the Stalin-sponsored 'General Line'. As he remarked at the January 1933 plenum of the Central Committee: "This is war!"[1] But Stalin was still seen in many high circles more as the sponsor of true Communist policies than as an infallible leader.

In the crucial period of 1931–1932, when victory over the peasants still hung in the balance, "loyalty to Stalin . . . was based principally on the conviction that there was no one to take his place, that any change of leadership would be extremely dangerous, since to stop now or attempt a retreat would mean to lose everything."[2] Or, as even a Trotskyite could comment, "If it were not for that so-and-so . . . everything would have fallen to pieces by now. It is he who keeps everything together."[3]

But even in those dangerous times, there were points on which Kirov, and others, felt free to oppose Stalin. Above all, this is true of Stalin's efforts in September 1932 to procure the execution of Ryutin. The latter and his group had circulated the 'Ryutin platform', which called for Stalin's ouster and a retreat from collectivization. This, and especially the first, was in Stalin's view treason. But Kirov and other leaders saw it as merely hostile factionalism, and recalled Lenin's appeal not to shed the blood of Bolsheviks. Kirov is reported as speaking 'with special force' against execution, and was supported by Ordzhonikidze, Kuibyshev, Kossior, and Kalinin. Only Kaganovich was on Stalin's side unreservedly, and the others wavered. In the end, Ryutin was imprisoned. This account, long unofficial, is now confirmed by Moscow.[4]

Stalin also attempted 'reprisals' against the Georgian Communist A. M. Nazaretyan, who had served with Kirov on the Transcaucasian Bureau[5] and had 'repeatedly' written attacking the excesses of collectivization. Again Kirov, with Ordzhonikidze and Kuibyshev, saved him.[6] There was further trouble in January 1933, when a group of Old Bolsheviks headed by the distinguished A. P. Smirov had discussed the removal of Stalin. As Stalin put it, "Of course, only enemies could say that to remove Stalin would not affect matters."[7] Kirov (a recent Soviet publication tells us) again strongly resisted a proposal that they should be shot, put forward by Stalin's point man Kaganovich, and won a majority.[8]

This was settled at the Central Committee plenum of January 1933. It took place in conditions of extreme terror, in the middle of the crisis due to the terror-famine now at its height in the Ukraine and other territories. Even in the Russian cities, bread supplies were very poor, and malnutrition affected the productivity and the morale of the population. There was a mood of crisis among the Central Committee members. Terekhov, First Secretary of the Kharkov Provincial Committee, brought the famine, hitherto always ritually denied, into the open.[9] Another speaker is reported as interrupting Kaganovich with, "But in our region they've started eating people!" Kaganovich replied "If we don't get hold of ourselves, you and I will be eaten . . . will that be better?"[10]

Thus, in spite of a feeling that Stalin's leadership had been disastrous, "at the same time, everyone realized that the fate of the regime was hanging by a thread, and any false step would lead to catastrophic ruin to all. None of them wanted such ruin. This forced them to close ranks, though they were all looking for a way out of the situation."[11] It was in this atmosphere that a 'Kirov line' started to emerge as an alternative to Stalin's—not so much while the emergency lasted, but as a determination for better tactics in the future.[12] And by mid-1933 it became clear that victory had been won. The country had become 'socialist'. The market economy no longer existed. The peasants were now state-controlled kolkhozniks, no longer 'petty-bourgeois' small proprietors.

The harvest was unexpectedly large, and "for the first time, wide circles of the membership [of the Party] came to believe that the 'general line' could be really successful."[13]

In Leningrad, as elsewhere, the new regime had settled down. A foreign Communist describes life in the Party House, where Kirov and other leaders lived, as already—no more indeed than in Moscow—"permeated with the spirit of hierarchy and class" and, though united against outsiders, a scene of "insidious and malevolent spite." The men kept up a political air of contact with the masses. The women simply indulged themselves, while doing 'social work'. The children had not even that amount of political consciousness, and were either frankly elitist or rebellious against the official ethic.[14] "Kirov's office in no way recalled the atmosphere of the enthusiasm of the October Revolution. Kirov himself, by his manner and methods reminded me of the cultured high officials of the Austrian administration I had known in Brünn, where, during the War, I had dealings with matters concerning Austrian refugees."[15]

Kirov's office, devoid of philistine and propagandist adornments, is described by a former oppositionist as being unlike that of a top party boss. It might rather have been the office of an engineer or a geologist. On the massive writing desk lay a variety of samples, models of oil-tanks, details of machines.[16]

In the view of Kirov and many other Bolsheviks, victory logically meant a relaxation of the dictatorship. The enemy classes had been destroyed. At the same time, the opposition Communist factions had been proved wrong; and, once they had confessed that this was so, they could be reintegrated into the Party.

As we have said, in the earlier period of intense intra-Party disagreements, the most heated polemics had often ended when the particular issue was settled. (Indeed, the two leading contestants might find themselves as friends and allies within months, as in the case of Lenin's fierce dispute with Trotsky over the role of Trade Unions in the early years of the regime.) Zinoviev and

Kamenev had been expelled and then readmitted to the Party in the late 1920s. Expelled again in 1932, this time for discussing the Ryutin Platform (another sign that a serious purge based on the Ryutin case was intended), they were again readmitted in 1933, and given posts.

Bukharin, Rykov, and Tomsky, the Rightist leaders, had never been expelled from the Party and had submitted to the General Line; and they had remained candidate members of the Central Committee. Bukharin, as director of industrial research, worked closely with Ordzhonikidze, head of the Supreme Economic Council and Commissar of Heavy Industry. By 1932 Bukharin had become a member of that commissariat's collegium and of the Commission for Formulating the new Five Year Plan.[17] And he was, in 1934, Chief Editor of *Izvestiya*. Rykov was Commissar for Posts and Telegraphs.

Bukharin and Kirov had remained on friendly terms in spite of some fierce political exchanges.[18] And, on the other flank, Kirov personally welcomed the ex-Trotskyite Sosnovsky to Leningrad, and kept up good relations with him.[19]

That Kirov encouraged ex-oppositionists to serve the Party is well established.[20] He also supported heretical literary figures on a number of occasions.[21] More significant still, from the point of view of our story, is the fact that he allowed some of the oppositionist Komsomol leaders, now restored to party membership but not to office, to carry out research for a history of the Leningrad Komsomol for the Party Institute.[22] Another ex-Zinovievite, Mikhail Khanik, as an engineer, received personal support from Kirov.[23] Sosnovsky also, working at his old trade of journalism, saw Kirov occasionally. In Kirov's office he once noticed a course on "The Resistance of Materials," and said to Kirov that he thought him more interested in the resistance of the class enemy. Kirov replied that the resistance of materials was just as important, and nowadays in fact even more so.[24]

A recent Soviet publication, in fictional form but passed by the censor and presumably an acceptable present-day analysis of the situation, tells us that Stalin was dissatisfied with Kirov for not wanting to join in "the struggle to strengthen the party leadership."[25]

Kirov is represented as saying to Stalin that the oppositionists are now reconciled to their defeat and have accepted the situation. Stalin strongly rebuts him, adding that "there are many Zinovievite roots in Leningrad."[26]

Kirov replies that in 1925 most of the local party rank and file only voted for the Zinovievites because of Party discipline.

Stalin accuses him of liberalism, and calls Leningrad "an as yet undestroyed bulwark of the opposition," and Kirov "a man who does not want to destroy this bastion."

Kirov, in turn, replies that Lenin favored reconciliation with defeated oppositionists, as the best way to disarm them. Kirov (the writer concludes) supported Stalin's line, but distrusted his personality, and regarded it as wrongly tending to "sharpen the intra-Party struggle."[27] At any rate, a strong disagreement between the two is indicated on an issue which was to be the main concern of Soviet politics over the years that followed.

Kirov's attitude on a reconciliation with the peasantry is also relevant. On this issue, too, an official biographer notes that he had no "opinion on collectivization" different from that of the Party, but that he yet took a comparatively moderate line.[28] And by early 1934, a tendency on his part to a more conciliatory policy to the peasants was noted by others.[29] He had, as we have seen, been one of the toughest proponents of the General Line against the "class enemy"; and those Soviet writers who speak of his turn to reconciliation with the country and the opposition are clear about this.[30]

As the leader in Leningrad, Kirov also had responsibility for a huge swathe from the Estonian border to the Arctic Ocean—and this included the notorious Baltic–White Sea Canal Project, started in 1930 and opened in May 1933. Between 200,000 and 300,000 forced laborers, mostly deported "kulaks" whose ranks were constantly replenished, hacked out the canal under appalling conditions. The deaths are reckoned at around 200,000. And the canal was in fact never of much use. Even small naval craft were too big for it, though some midget submarines were transferred on barges between the two seas. Little is now heard of it, though a low-grade Soviet cigarette called "Belomorkanal" still carries on its packet a map showing not only this canal but two other similar Stalinist slave-labor projects—the Moscow–Volga and the Volga–Don canals. In July 1933, Kirov, Stalin, and Voroshilov went on a ceremonial trip up part of it, and Stalin effusively congratulated and embraced Kirov.[31] (Kirov is, however, reported as saying that the handling of big construction projects by the police was uneconomic and unprofitable.)[32]

But, more generally, as one observer noted, the very fact that Kirov could not be accused of undue tenderness, "added to his strength in the official circles in which he had to defend his point of view,"[33] as he now began to do. As a former Leningrad journalist wrote, in 1934 Kirov had "won the reputation of a liberal, though earlier he had not been inclined to liberalism."[34]

Thus, in one way or another Kirov began to represent an inchoate tendency to reconciliation within the Party and between the Party and the population.

For the moment, and up to a point, Stalin accepted the mood. He himself remarked at the XVII Congress, in February 1934:

> Whereas at the XV Congress it was still necessary to prove the correctness of the Party line and to fight certain anti-Leninist groupings, and at the XVI Congress to finish off the last supporters of these groupings, at the present Congress there is nothing to prove and, it seems, nobody to beat.

And the former oppositionists, the Rightists Bukharin and Rykov, Zinoviev and Kamenev, and the ex-Trotskyites Pyatakov and Radek were Congress speakers, affirming the new unanimity. And when Rakovsky, the last of the prominent Trotskyites to hold out against reconciliation, made his peace with the Party in March 1934, he was welcomed at the station by Kaganovich—a further signal that Stalin was now, at least publicly, in accord with this 'moderate' political line.

Stalin in fact needed all his skills of maneuver. The XVII Congress was a critical point. Whatever his professions, many leading Bolsheviks had come to think that, however necessary in the crises of 1930–1933, he was not the man to lead the Party into a period of internal reconciliation. And at the Congress, official accounts published in the 1960s tell us:

A number of delegates of the Congress, and above all those who remembered Lenin's testament, considered that the time had come to remove Stalin from the post of secretary general to transfer him to another function, because, certain of his infallibility, he was beginning to ignore the principle of collective work, and was again becoming rude.[35]

This version is confirmed by two leading samizdat historians of the 1970s.[36]

We are told that a group of senior delegates assembled to discuss the matter. M. D. Orakhelashvili (Kirov's old colleague in the Caucasus) and G. I. Petrovsky figure in both accounts, while the group is also reported as including S. V. Kossior, Sheboldayev, Eikhe, and Ordzhonikidze (in whose apartment the talk, or one of the talks, is said to have taken place). I. M. Vareikis is also mentioned as a leading figure in connection with the proposal of Kirov as the new General Secretary—plausibly enough, as he too had served with him in Astrakhan[37] and the Caucasus.[38]

Our accounts agree that Kirov refused the proposal.[39] The grounds he gave were politically understandable: "If I was made General Secretary that would signify putting in question the whole policy of the party—collectivization, industrialization, nationality policy, our construction of socialism in general. No, I should not agree to that."[40]

Of course, the whole discussion between these senior delegates reached Stalin, and it cannot have pleased him.[41] On one account, moreover, Kirov himself told Stalin that though he himself had rejected the idea of becoming General Secretary on political grounds, nevertheless, "You yourself are to blame for what happened. After all, we told you things couldn't be done in such a drastic way."[42]

The delegates now elected the new Central Committee; and even to that body Stalin's candidature was strongly opposed (in secret ballot).

The samizdat historians, while differing in some details, tell us that 270 (or 289) delegates (out of 1,966) actually voted against Stalin (as the number of names on the ballot was the same as the number to be elected this meant that his name had actually to be crossed out).[43] They recount how the vice-chairman of the elec-

toral commission, V. M. Verkhovykh, later described to the 1957
Commission of Enquiry how Kaganovich ordered the Chairman,
Zatonsky, to change this to three against. (This was the same
number as had voted against Kirov!) The 1957 Commission also
elicited supporting evidence from another survivor of the electoral
commission, who gave it most reluctantly, as tending to under-
mine Stalin's authority.[44] This account was moreover confirmed
in its essentials by Khrushchev.[45]

In the years that followed, 1,108 of the 1,966 delegates were
shot as enemies of the people.[46]

L. S. Shaumyan, one of the few surviving delegates, wrote in
Pravda in the 1960s that Stalin had understood that his efforts
to seize supreme power were "meeting a decisive obstacle in the
form of the old Leninist cadres of the party," going on to speak
in particular of "that fine Leninist, S. M. Kirov."[47]

So the evidence remained until late 1987 when (on 13 December 1987), in an interesting confirmation of the oblique or
unofficial information on which we often have to rely, a Soviet periodical printed a section of Mikoyan's memoirs hitherto unpublished. Mikoyan now revealed that Kirov had indeed got just under
300 more votes at the XVII Congress than Stalin did; that a group
of delegates approached him with a view to his becoming General
Secretary; that he refused; and that he "told Stalin and was met
with hostility and a will to revenge against the whole Congress
and of course Kirov personally."[48]

What might have ensued if Kirov had become General Secretary?

Politically, he had proved himself an exceedingly able tactician.
There is little to show that he was capable of ruling the country.
He is described as unsuitable because "not a theoretician but a
practical revolutionary."[49] On the other hand, his appointment
as General Secretary might have meant the emergence of something in the nature of a genuine collective leadership with a division of authority and reduction of the Secretariat's power to a
lower level of intensity.

As it was, he was now elected a Secretary of the Central Committee. Stalin wanted him to give up his Leningrad post and come
to Moscow. After some argument, he was allowed to keep both

posts, and to remain in Leningrad until the end of the Second Five Year Plan—that is into 1938.[50] Meanwhile, he remained a possible alternative to the Stalin leadership, as "the initiator of that modest, almost unnoticed, liberalisation, which began after the Seventeenth Party Congress."[51]

In foreign affairs, too, Western scholars have noted a certain apparent divergence from the Stalin line.[52] The traditional Bolshevik policy of collaboration with the German army was deepset. But Hitler's accession to power at the beginning of 1933, though at first expected by the Communists to be temporary, was soon seen as menacing. However, at the XVII Congress Stalin said that fascism in Germany was in itself no barrier to good state relations with the USSR, such as Fascist Italy already enjoyed. Contact was maintained. And it is clear from all our sources that through 1934–1935 he and his closest colleagues (in particular Molotov and Kaganovich) let the Germans know of Soviet hopes in that direction. Radek, close to Stalin, clearly favored it, and junior officials were allowed to be, discreetly, almost effusive about Nazism.

The trouble was, rather, that Hitler at this point appeared intransigently anti-Soviet. By mid-1934 Stalin was hedging his bets, and Communist Parties were beginning to urge 'United Fronts' with their Socialist counterparts—(while maintaining, and in the most public fashion, their intention of becoming the most influential, and then the dominant element in the fronts). In the sphere of state relations too, Stalin played the card of rapprochement with France.

That the commitment against Nazism was not absolute became clear with the Nazi–Soviet Pact of 1939: but this pact was only possible because for some years Stalin, while publicly pursuing the antifascist line, had kept this option open in confidential contacts in Berlin. In fact, he certainly felt that the rapprochement with the West was valuable at one level as a means of getting a better bargain with the Nazis, should they prove amenable.

The Comintern line on Nazism, and 'fascism' in general, had been that it was one of two manifestations of bourgeois mobilization for the class struggle, the other being 'social democracy', usually characterized as 'social-fascism'. (A recent article by a veteran Soviet diplomat discusses the divergence between Stalin and Bukharin on this issue.[53]) Social democracy was originally represented as the main enemy. Indeed, even in Germany itself, the Communists had sometimes overtly collaborated with the Nazis against the moderate parties, as in the Prussian referendum of 1931 and the Transport Strike of 1932.

Thus from Stalin's point of view Nazism was of course hostile to Communism: but so were all other 'bourgeois' parties and states. The argument advanced by Bukharin that Nazism was against 'humanism' could carry no weight. The question was simply a practical one. Did Germany present a threat? If so, could it be diverted? Could the equally unacceptable democracies be used against Hitler? Or, alternatively, could Hitler be used against the democracies?

But Bukharin, and it seems to some degree at least Kirov as well, envisaged a more humane Soviet order and saw Nazism as the doctrinal enemy of such a development. Thus they could envisage at least some Soviet convergence with 'bourgeois democracy'. (Or, in another interpretation, they realized that, even if hypocritical, the 'democratic' ideas held in the West might yet be usable in the struggle against antihumane fascism.)

The Italian scholar Francesco Benvenuti has shown that Kirov made a number of speeches attacking the Nazis and the Japanese, of which the fiercest passages were omitted in the version given in *Pravda*.[54] We are told that in private, too, Kirov expressed alarm at the "possibility of war with fascist Germany."[55]

In this context of different policy approaches, with Stalin not fully committed to either, there is certainly a variation, at least in emphasis, between some of Kirov's speeches and others made by Kaganovich and others. The divergence should perhaps be seen as Stalin consciously permitting a certain variety of arguments by subordinates before final decisions were taken.

And since Stalin was able to pursue policies of the People's Front and of the Western Alliance precisely through the worst period of the Terror, it is clear that no linkage to internal democratization of the type Bukharin and others may have desired was necessary.

Nevertheless, at least to the extent that some such feeling was in the air, Kirov's tendency seems to have been in that general direction. It seems probable that, like Bukharin, Kirov saw not only that Hitler was anti-Communist, but that he represented an unappeasable threat at the level of state policy. One may nevertheless feel that international considerations were of secondary importance compared with the urgent issues of internal policy.

Out of the public eye, Kirov was now constantly in disagreement with Moscow.

This struggle, and the disputes in which he became involved, were, as far as outside observers were concerned, conducted in almost complete silence. Even now our knowledge of what went on is only partial. But there is no doubt that the main political issue of 1934 was whether Stalin would be able, by one means or another, to overcome the powerful tendencies in the party of which Kirov had come to be the representative.

One of several issues on which they quarreled was the rationing system in Leningrad. Kirov maintained that workers worked better if they got more food; Stalin upheld the contrary argument: Why should Leningrad do better than other cities? Quarrels on this point are reported both by a defector[56] and by Khrushchev, who tells us that when Kirov's spokesman (evidently P. A. Irklis)[57] reported on this to the Politburo, Stalin afterwards made highly offensive remarks, and Khrushchev himself witnessed "an exchange of sharp words between Stalin and Sergei Kirov."[58] And, Mikoyan tells us, Stalin sponsored such pinpricks as a condemnation by the Politburo of an "unfortunate" phrase in an article Kirov had published back in 1913.[59]

On the agricultural side, there was a dispute on the role of the Machine Tractor Stations, whose 'political sections' were Stalin's great instrument of control over village life, and an obstacle to detente in the villages. This is confirmed by a former Leningrad party journalist.[60] And Kirov is also reported as actively opposing a case brought by the NKVD against a group of agronomists.[61]

It is also told of him that he rebuffed Stalin's prize journalist Mikhail Kol'tsov, when the latter, in the tradition of Stalinist journalism, tried publicly to inculpate some of his subordinates; but indirect slurs on his rule in Leningrad appeared—and, as Mikoyan tells us, could not have done so without Stalin's direct approval.[62] But it was, of course, not only a matter of Stalin. If moderates— including Kirov—were prepared to overlook Stalin's faults because of what they felt to be his merits, this did not apply to Kaganovich, Yezhov and the others. Any change in the regime would mean the end of their careers. They resisted strongly.[63] (Kirov is described as "extremely hostile to Kaganovich."[64])

At the same time that Stalin felt constrained to accept the political relaxation, he began to build up machinery suited to an eventual policy of repression—in fact to the one he actually pursued over the following years. In July 1934 the OGPU was abolished and a new All-Union NKVD took over its, and other, powers. Genrikh G. Yagoda became the People's Commissar and Ya. S. Agranov, a close confidant of Stalin, his Deputy. Over the previous year a Party Purge Commission had been formed, which included Nikolai Yezhov, later to win such dreadful international fame. Yezhov was also made Head of the key Personnel Department of the Central Committee, and of the Party Control Commission. At the same time, he headed the Industrial Department.

A more secret 'Special Sector' of the Central Committee, headed by Stalin's secretary Aleksandr Poskrebyshev, also seems to have been founded about this time, together with an extralegal State Security Committee that included Yezhov, Agranov, Poskrebyshev, and others.

In the summer of 1934 Stalin called Kirov to Sochi. There he proposed that he should go to Kazakhstan as the Politburo's representative to bring in the critical harvest; and then go to Moscow.[65] Kirov, however, repeated that he would stay in Leningrad until the end of the Second Five Year Plan in 1938. This may perhaps be regarded as the moment when Stalin, if still toying with the idea of neutralizing Kirov in the capital, felt obliged to think again. Kirov spent almost all September in Kazakhstan[66] where he tried to restore the ruined countryside (after the disastrous years in which at least a quarter of the local population had died and rural production had been ruined). While in Kazakhstan, he had a car accident, which has been interpreted as an assassination attempt.[67] He was back in Leningrad within weeks, to face further trouble.

The 1987 Soviet account in fictional form which we have already quoted (pp. 25–26) says that Leningrad's NKVD Chief F. D. Medved reported to Kirov in September 1934 that I. V. Zaporozhets, his deputy, acting without his knowledge or permission, had brought in people from the central NKVD apparat in Moscow and given them key posts in the local Secret Political Department. Medved said this was impermissible, since it meant two NKVD chiefs in Leningrad, one responsible to the Provincial Committee and the other to Moscow. Medved demanded the removal of both Zaporozhets and his new men.

The question (this account continues) was sensitive. Indubitably, these appointments had been sanctioned. Probably, they had been made on the direct instructions of Stalin to "uproot the remnants of the opposition," in defiance of Kirov—" 'You don't want to do it, I'll do it without you' " which is why Zaporozhets was was thus showing his independence. To seek the recall of Zaporozhets would mean direct conflict with Stalin on a delicate cadre question in which Stalin would permit no such intervention.[68]

Kirov nevertheless calls a meeting of the bureau of the Provincial Committee, and has Medved repeat his story. The bureau then votes unanimously for the immediate recall of Zaporozhets and his men.

Kirov next telephones Stalin, who asks what exactly Zaporozhets is supposed to have done wrong. Kirov replies that he has brought in these five men from Yagoda's Central NKVD without Medved's permission. Stalin retorts that this is an internal matter for the NKVD. Kirov angrily asks what about his own position as Leningrad Provincial Secretary. Stalin answers that this is puerile: the NKVD was a new Commissariat, and it was not practically possible to clear all appointments in this way. Kirov repeats his and the Leningrad bureau's demand for Zaporozhets's removal, to which Stalin answers that he has explained matters and can do no more and thereupon hangs up.[69] Kirov tells Medved that he has done what he can, and if this division of powers between him and Zaporozhets causes trouble, he will support Medved.[70]

This fictional account, though published in 1987, was written twenty years earlier, and is based, perhaps not with perfect accuracy, on material then being presented to the Commission set up by Khrushchev to investigate the Kirov murder. Some of this, with other similar material, had already been referred to in samizdat, including reports by several witnesses who claim that Kirov was already in fear of his life. One of these was his Old Bolshevik sister-in-law, another an old colleague, another a well-known official.[71]

If Kirov's apprehensions were as reported, it is unclear whether he saw the threat as coming from Stalin himself, or from others of the Stalinist persuasion. But it was only just over thirty years since a Russian Prime Minister, Petr Stolypin, had been assassinated by an agent of his own Secret Police, having earlier expressed a fear that this might happen.

A few days before his death Kirov and the other Leningrad members attended the plenum of the Central Committee on 25–28 November in Moscow to which we referred in Chapter I. The 'Kirov line' on relaxation was, in effect, accepted at this plenum. Its main resolution was on the abolition of bread rationing,[72] which actually took place in January 1935. Stalin in fact continued to follow the line of relaxation in areas where it did not affect political power. For example, it was Stalin who now suggested the drafting of a new Soviet Constitution. This document, composed mostly by Bukharin, was to be a model of liberalism and democracy. Bukharin himself thought it would really begin to give a measure of liberty and reconciliation to the country.[73]

The Constitution actually came into effect in 1936, just as the new Terror got under way. It confused Westerners as well as Russians. The "Noon" of Arthur Koestler's *Darkness at Noon* represents the new vision apparently embodied in the Constitution. The great British cartoonist Low did a famous drawing of a baffled Western onlooker viewing a Soviet Union half in glowing sunshine with happiness and freedom, labelled "New Constitution," and half in darkness, with sinister figures carrying out obscure deeds beneath a label about the latest confession trials.

The genuine attempt at reconciliation within the Party, and between the Party and the population, for which Kirov had lately worked, was foreclosed when he fell on 1 December 1934. In fact, his death became the official reason for its destruction. What might, rather broadly, be described as Kirov's heritage was thus to be accepted in form, but sabotaged in practice.

CHAPTER V

Stalin Interrogates

As soon as Kirov was shot, Chudov had telephoned Stalin with the news. That very evening, a decree was issued which laid down that in cases of terrorism:

1. Investigation agencies are directed to speed up the cases of those accused of the preparation or execution of acts of terror.
2. Judicial organs are directed not to hold up the execution of death sentences pertaining to crimes of this category in order to consider the possibility of pardon, since the Central Executive Committee of the USSR does not consider as possible the receiving of petitions of this sort.
3. The organs of the NKVD are directed to execute the death sentence against criminals of the above category immediately after the passing of sentences.

A prominent and highly intelligent East European Communist stationed in Moscow (whom the present author chanced to know personally, as a minister in his own country a good many years later), told an American diplomat that "an act of terror of this kind at this particular moment could trigger acts of repression on the part of the Soviet regime that would make even the collectivisation campaign of 1930 look mild. He said that for some time

Stalin had been angered at the latest opposition to his policies that existed in various quarters." He added that the decree of 1 December "was an indication of what might be expected."[1]

We are told that the Politburo approved of this decree "casually," only after it had been published.[2] On 10 December new articles of the Code of Criminal Procedure of the Russian Socialist Federal Soviet Republic (RSFSR) were passed to regularize it. It was to prove a charter of terror over the years that followed. The whole Soviet press was full of obituaries to Kirov, coupled with very strong threats of vengeance against the enemy, in the tone of the Red Terror of 1918 following the attempt on Lenin's life.

As soon as arrangements could be made, Stalin set out for Leningrad with a high-level political and police presence to make a personal investigation. It was officially announced that Stalin, with Molotov and Voroshilov of the Politburo and Zhdanov of the Secretariat—all thorough Stalinists—formed the delegation proper.[3]

They were accompanied by others of a lower heirarchical level, but sometimes of greater significance in the case. These included A. V. Kosarev, General Secretary of the Komsomol; G. G. Yagoda, NKVD People's Commissar; Ya. S. Agranov, Yagoda's Deputy People's Commissar in charge of State Security; and N. I. Yezhov.[4] Yezhov took with him V. E. Tsesarsky, his chief assistant at the Industrial Department of the Central Committee, which at this time was another of his responsibilities.[5] (Tsesarsky later became a leading figure in the NKVD.) Stalin's secretary Poskrebyshev is also reported, as would be natural. So is Andrei Vyshinsky, then Deputy Prosecutor of the USSR, who was certainly there later in the month.[6]

Agranov brought with him a high-level state security team, which included (apparently) L. G. Mironov, Head of the NKVD Economic Department; and (certainly) G. S. Lyuskhov, Deputy Head of the Secret Political Department; A. I. Volovich, Deputy Head of the Operative Department; D. M. Dmitriev, a senior interrogator in the Secret Political Department; and an array of subordinates.[7]

But until the arrival of the people from Moscow, Nikolayev was of course in the hands of the Leningrad NKVD; that is, of the body which, as we have seen, had proved itself incompetent, and something suspiciously more than incompetent, in protecting Kirov's life.

For even as to the facts known to Chudov and the others, there was something dubious about the actions of the Leningrad NKVD, or some members of it. The absence of all guards at the Smolny was, on the face of it, an astonishing lapse, and so was the failure of Kirov's bodyguard to accompany him.

F. D. Medved, as head of the Leningrad NKVD, had as his Deputies I. V. Zaporozhets (on the State Security side) and F. T. Fomin. Medved, like most senior police officials, had a ruthless past in Leningrad, Byelorussia, the Far East, and elsewhere. He had achieved special renown for cases against leading church figures—as with the Metropolitans Antonin and Aleksei in the late twenties.[8]

Zaporozhets, we are told, had been a member of the Left Social Revolutionary Party, but had gone over to the Bolsheviks. Joining the Cheka, he had infiltrated the staff of the Anarchist commander Makhno—dangerous work. He is described as "tall, broad shouldered, a 'fine figure of a man' . . . a joker and a wit, the life of the party at picnics and outings, and a connoisseur of wine and women. Full of the joy of life. . . ."[9] In the 1930s he had worked under Yagoda as deputy head of the OGPU Information Department, and became a trusted aide of the secret police chief; and he was also on friendly terms with Agranov.[10] He was a delegate from Leningrad to the XVII Party Congress so he must already have been promoted to Deputy Head of that city's secret police.[11] His wife, Proskurovskaya, is reported joining the staff of the Leningrad Provincial Committee.[12] As it turned out—and as is agreed by all sources, Stalinist and anti-Stalinist—it had been on Zaporozhets's order that Nikolayev, after his two arrests in Kirov's neighborhood with a revolver, had twice been released—against the protests of those on guard duty.

The security side of the Leningrad NKVD which Zaporozhets headed was divided into departments representing the central operational departments of the Main Administration of State Security (GUGB) in Moscow. These were the *Secret Political Department,* covering anti-Soviet organizations; the *Special Department,* also concerned with the registration of plots, and with

army matters; the *Operative Department,* in charge of the security
of high officials; the *Transport Department;* the *Economic Department;* and the *Foreign Department.* Apart from the Economic
and Transport Departments, these were all in one way or another
involved in the case—the Foreign Department because it oversaw
all foreign contacts, including that of Nikolayev's wife with the
Latvian consulate.

The Secret Political Department, as was to be expected of any
moderately efficient security service, had long since been aware of
Nikolayev's attitudes and threats.[13] They had reported this to
Zaporozhets. And Zaporozhets had got in touch with Nikolayev
through one of the latters' friends, an informant for the police.[14]
One account has it that Zaporozhets arranged for a revolver to be
provided, and had his agent persuade Nikolayev to attempt the
assassination not of a member of the local Control Commission,
his original target, but Kirov.[15]

Zaporozhets himself was, however, on leave in the South when
the assassination occurred.[16]

When Nikolayev was arrested, Fomin was present, and later
described how he was the first to interrogate the assassin. Nikolayev said nothing, only asking for some money, found in the
search of his flat, to be passed to his wife and his mother. According to Fomin, Nikolayev wept and vomited—the latter the result
of having drunk a good deal of beer.[17]

Bal'tsevich, of the Leningrad NKVD Operative Department, and
responsible for Smolny guard duties, is another officer we know
who took part in the interrogation at this point.[18] Other officers
searched Nikolayev's flat and arrested relatives and acquaintances.

A number of documents were found in Nikolayev's briefcase or
in his apartment: "a diary, statements addressed to various institutions, etc."[19] From them, as we have seen, it was evident that his
crime was "a personal act of desperation and dissatisfaction" and
a protest against "the unjust attitude of certain members of the
government towards a live person."[20] The above was entered into
the interrogation record at once—it is on page 6 of its Volume 1.
This entry later became an embarrassment to the 'investigation'.

A worse embarrassment, however, seems to have arisen some
time before the Muscovites arrived. One report has it that an

NKVD officer who had actually had contact with Nikolayev in the guise of a sympathetic civilian, now hoped to bully a confession out of him by a direct confrontation, on the miscalculation that he was a broken man in a helpless and hopeless position, who would do what he was told. The source has Zaporozhets as the officer.[21] This is evidently an error, as Zaporozhets was almost certainly not in Leningrad during 2 December. But the report may be a distorted reference to one of Zaporozhets's accomplices (possibly, as we shall see, Bal'tsevich).

At any rate it is clear from several accounts that at some point during the interrogation, and before the arrival of the Moscow investigators, Nikolayev had become fully aware of the part played by the NKVD[22]—including, apparently, the role of his 'friend', the police agent, under whose guidance he had practiced shooting "since August."[23]

We are told that Stalin and the others got to Leningrad "fifteen or sixteen hours" after the assassination, that is, around 7:30–8:30 A.M. on 2 December;[24] or, on another account "at the crack of dawn."[25]

Stalin and the major figures went to the Smolny. As with Tsar Nicholas I's interrogation of the Decembrists, he had the accused brought before him personally.

As is usual in these cases, there is some divergence of evidence as to who else was present at this interrogation. Stalin, Voroshilov, Molotov, Zhdanov, and Kosarev, with a number of Leningrad officials headed by Chudov and a group of NKVD officers, seem best attested.[26]

When Nikolayev was brought in, Stalin is reported as quietly asking why he had shot Kirov.[27] All accounts agree that Nikolayev replied boldly, pointing to the NKVD men and saying that Stalin should ask *them* that question. He was thereupon silenced and removed.[28]

Stalin is also reported to have interrogated Nikolayev's relations, and perhaps others. According to one detailed account, impossible to confirm (and certainly wrong as to things heard second-hand), Stalin also interrogated a nonpolitical but former 'White' woman whose name had been found in Nikolayev's diary—with a view, presumably, to establishing a 'White' terrorist connection.[29]

At any rate, Stalin was "present at certain of the more important interrogations."[30]

These suspects were brought from NKVD headquarters to the Smolny, where Stalin and the informal board of inquiry remained. Agranov, at his side, arranged for these people to be sent over.

One of those whose testimony was clearly required was Borisov, head of Kirov's guard.

Accounts are agreed that Borisov was devoted to Kirov, and that he had immediately become suspicious when he and his men had arrested Nikolayev twice with a revolver, and found him released each time. By now he must have deduced the arrangements of Zaporozhets and the others. His testimony to the commission could have been of no benefit to Stalin, and indeed was almost bound to be thoroughly troublesome. Nikolayev's testimony was bad enough, but he at least was a criminal who could be labelled a half-crazed slanderer. Borisov could not.

Late in the morning of 2 December, Volovich, at Leningrad NKVD headquarters, was instructed on the telephone by Agranov to send Borisov to the Smolny.[31]

Volovich sent Borisov in a truck. One NKVD man sat with the driver, and Borisov and two other NKVD men were in the back. They are described as members of Stalin's guard[32] (i.e., Volovich's own men from the central Operative Department). As the truck went along Voinov Street, the NKVD man in front seized the steering wheel and the truck hit a warehouse wall, though not very hard.[33] It was then stated that Borisov had been killed in the accident. He had in fact been killed by his guards, with iron bars.[34] This version is common, as we shall see, to the later Stalinist and the post-Stalinist official accounts. The killers in the truck were themselves later liquidated.[35]

The Leningrad NKVD were still apparently working with their superiors from Moscow at this time in the late morning of 2 December, when A. S. Gorin is reported present with Volovich and Lyushkov in the local NKVD headquarters, using Medved's office.[36] But during the day,[37] almost the whole leadership of the Leningrad NKVD—with the extraordinary exception of Zaporezhets—

were removed from their posts and sent for trial for "negligence in connection with their duties."[38] The following were named:

F. D. Medved: Head of the Leningrad NKVD

F. T. Fomin: Deputy Head

A. S. Gorin: described by Lyushkov as Head of the Special Department[39]

P. M. Lobov: believed to be Head of the Secret Political Department[39]

D. I. Yanishevsky: believed to be Head of the International Department[40]

G. A. Petrov: believed to be an officer of the Special Department

M. S. Bal'tsevich: believed to be Head or Deputy Head of the Operative Department[41]

A. A. Mosevich: later held a post as Head of the Dalstroy Secret Political Department, so possibly he had served in the same Department in Leningrad.

Agranov was given temporary charge of the Leningrad NKVD.[42] And new men took over as his subordinates. For instance P. A. Korkin became head of the Leningrad Secret Political Department.[43]

Stalin had arrived on 2 December, and he left again two days later, so he only had a limited time to develop the case. (And part of the time he had to join the honorary guard at Kirov's coffin, with Chudov representing Leningrad). The case had not so far gone usefully, and he is reported to have shown anger at Yagoda—who returned to Moscow before the others, in a chastened mood.[44]

As Stalin and his senior colleagues returned to Moscow, he put Yezhov in political control of the case with Agranov running the actual investigation. They continued to receive detailed instructions from the General Secretary.[45]

On Stalin's return a meeting of the Politburo still saw a majority, to which Stalin acceded, to continue the planned economic reforms. On the other hand, the assassination was to be made the occasion for a purge of the Party's ranks while the case itself was left to the investigating authorities.[46]

Kirov's coffin arrived in Moscow at 10:30 A.M. on 4 December, and the State funeral started at 2:30 P.M. on 6 December. Stalin was again one of the guards of honor.

CHAPTER VI

The First Victims

While Agranov pursued his enquiries in a manner we shall describe in the next chapter, the first executions under the terror-decree of 1 December were carried out.

On 4 December it was announced that "cases of recently arrested Whiteguards charged with preparing terrorist attacks against workers of the Soviet power" had been sent on 2 December for immediate consideration to the Military Collegium of the Supreme Court.[1] The period from 5 December to 18 December saw the announcement of the trial and execution of 102 of these 'Whiteguards'— in Leningrad and Moscow on 6 December, Minsk on 12 December, and Kiev on 18 December. (17 were remanded for "further investigation").

The Military Collegium, meeting in these cities, consisted of the names which became infamous in the great faked trials of 1936–1938. Above all V. V. Ulrikh, who chaired the court in Moscow and Kiev, I. O. Matulevich, who chaired it in Leningrad and Minsk, A. P. Goryachev, and N. M. Rychkov.

All those indicted were accused of being terrorists sent over the frontiers with arms and instructions to assassinate. The accused in Leningrad were said to have come "through Latvia and in part through Finland or Poland," those in Moscow "through Poland and in part Latvia," and in Kiev "the majority from Poland, some from

Rumania."[2] As we shall see, the charges are false where we can check them. Indeed, a former commander of NKVD border troops writes that he understood this at once, since terrorists do not cross frontiers "in droves."[3]

On the other hand, the deans of Western sociology, Sidney and Beatrice Webb, comment on these cases in their *Soviet Communism: A New Civilisation*. According to the Webbs, these "White-guards" did not seem to have been proved to be accomplices in the assassination "or the conspiracies associated therewith," but that they were "undoubtedly guilty of illegal entry and inexcusably bearing arms and bombs."[4] The evidence before the Webbs was, of course, the brief announcements to that effect in the Soviet press.

In Leningrad, Moscow, and Minsk, the names of the accused are hard to identify. The thirty-eight Leningrad victims are described as mostly from the remnants of the old ruling classes.[5] And the first named of the twenty-seven Moscow dead, R. Vasilev, is said to have been an economist, and former Social Revolutionary, a political prisoner in Tsarist times, who had been arrested in November.[6] The nine killed in Minsk are of unknown origin.

In Kiev, on the other hand, many of the victims were well-known figures, associated with the cultural revival of the Ukraine. The country's intelligentsia had already been repressed in a whole cycle of trials from 1930 onwards.[7]

The Ukrainians who were now sentenced (28 to death and 9 held for further investigation) were accused of having for the most part crossed the frontier "with revolvers and hand grenades." They included twenty-three well-known writers and cultural and social figures. Few of them had been abroad, apart from a former Soviet diplomat, M. M. Lebedynets, though seven were Western Ukrainians who had immigrated from that Polish-occupied territory.

All we know of the circumstances[8] of the arrests is that three of those shot had been arrested on minor charges early in 1934, but released on condition of moving out of the Ukraine to eastern areas of the USSR, being at liberty, and preparing to depart, as late as November.

Some of the more prominent names were not among those shot, including men who had indeed been members of non-Communist

parties before and during the Revolution: though their mere sur-
vival as late as this, when all such not regarded as adequately loyal
to the Soviet regime had long since been purged, tends to testify to
their innocence. (On the other hand, it can be argued that *all*
Ukrainian intellectuals, Communist or otherwise, were now at least
estranged from Moscow.)

P. F. Helmer-Didushok was an Ukrainian Social Democrat who
had been on that party's delegation to the Second International,
but had accepted and served the Soviet regime since 1920. Another, Yu. A. Bachynsky, a journalist, was also a former Social
Democrat, who had been Ukrainian envoy in Washington, accept-
ing the Soviet regime in the early thirties. The most distinguished
of this group, however, was the writer A. V. Khrushelnytsky,
former Minister of Education in the Ukrainian People's Republic,
who had also become reconciled to the Soviet regime. He too was
only sentenced to prison and sent to the notorious Solovki camp as
was his daughter, a doctor (not on trial), and he died some time
after 1937.[9] Both his sons, on trial with him, were among those
shot.

The playwright Vasyl Mysyk, aged twenty-seven, was not only
among the names listed but not shot: he actually served a long
sentence in Solovki,[10] and (unlike all the others named here) survived Stalin. In the 1960s his articles appeared in the literary
magazines; and he has an entry in the Soviet *Short Literary Ency-
lopaedia* (which lists his works, none appearing between 1933 and
1962). I have found only one Soviet reference to his experiences,
that his works "were doomed to oblivion in the years of the cult
of personality."[11]

Among the twenty-eight executed, however, we find K. S. Bur-
evy, a former Social Revolutionary imprisoned under the Tsars.
During the Civil War he had been Chairman of the Voronezh
Soviet, but later abandoned politics and became a playwright. His
plays were censored in 1932; but he had only been arrested in
November or December 1934, as were Pivnenko, Protsenko, and
Matyash, all also shot.[12] Hryhoriy Kosynka, a short-story writer
and son of a poor peasant, had fought for the independent Ukrai-
nian Republic and been arrested when the Bolsheviks seized the
Ukraine, though later released.[13] Dmytro Falkiwsky, poet, on the

other hand, had fought in the Red Army.[14] He was rehabilitated in the 1960s.[15]

The most remarkable figure among those shot was, however, the twenty-six-year-old deaf-and-dumb poet Oleksa Vlyzko. There was a rumor, or legend, in Kiev and the Ukraine that before he was shot he regained his voice, denounced the secret police, foretold the end of Moscow's domination in the Ukraine, and called for vengeance.[16] His poetry was described in 1935 as "a screen for bandit activity and a weapon for bandit assault and treacherous poisoning."[17] But in Khrushchev's time he too was rehabilitated. In his case alone, we have part of his alleged confession, appearing in a public speech by a Ukrainian Communist leader in 1935. He had, in 1929, "joined a Ukrainian fascist nationalist organization . . . I fully subscribed to all the terrorist precepts of the fascist platform."[18]

His and Falkiwsky's rehabilitations sufficiently prove that the case (including the confessions, if indeed they were actually made) was totally false.

These executions strongly, and no doubt consciously, parallel the 'Red Terror' shootings of August 1918, following the attempted assassination of Lenin by Fanny Kaplan. They, and their emphatic public announcement, contributed greatly to the impact of the ever-intensifying press campaign against enemies of the people.

This also manifested itself in Leningrad by the mass deportation of the survivors of the old classes. And, as we shall see, the campaign against the 'Whiteguard' terrorist organizations was to be linked to the next groups of victims from the Communist Party itself.

CHAPTER VII

The First Story:
The Leningrad Terrorist Center

The investigation, under Yezhov and Agranov's guidance, continued. It was not at first clear to the interrogators what direction it was supposed to take. It was not for some days that instructions came that the former Zinoviev opposision were to be implicated.[1]

The investigation proceeded in a peculiar atmosphere. It is clear that, while the Leningrad NKVD were in disgrace for incompetence, knowledge of the true nature of the conspiracy involving Zaporozhets was kept within as limited a circle as possible, in fact on a 'need to know' basis. It is fairly plain, for example, that Voroshilov knew nothing of it. Nor, apparently, did Lyushkov.

This must have made the atmosphere of the investigation rather strained, at least for those in the know. However, the commitment to involve the local ex-Zinovievites was a matter of routine brutality. The only sensitive point must have been the handling of Nikolayev himself with his awkward knowledge.

We need not imagine any difficulties of conscience on the part of the investigators. Major political 'investigations' had for years been falsified—the 'Shakhty' Trial of 1928, the Menshevik Case of 1931 (in which Dmitriev had been chief interrogator) and the Metro-Vic Trial of 1933 (which Mironov had conducted) were only the most striking examples. It is perfectly clear that in such situations, including this one, the interrogators set themselves the task not of discovering the truth, but of putting together a case to suit a political decision already taken,[2] as indeed one of them states flatly.[3]

In fact, as the Leninist dissident Roy Medvedev puts it, "the investigation was carried out in complete violation of the law, of common sense, of the desire to find and punish the real culprits."[4] The first to be arrested and interrogated were genuine contacts of Nikolayev's who, unlike others accused, are not described even in the Indictment as 'former members of the Zinoviev opposition':[5] I. G. Yuskin (said to have been a neighbor of Nikolayev's), N. S. Antonov, A. I. Tolmazov, V. I. Zvezdov, and G. V. Sokolov. (The earliest arrested certainly include Zvezdov and Sokolov, who appear, as none of the ex-Zinovievites do, in Volume I of the interrogation record.[6])

Nikolayev must have talked of his intentions to at least one other person, the informer of the Secret Political Department. Even if he did not go quite so far with most others, he surely spoke wildly and resentfully to some of his acquaintances of what he saw as the bureaucratic regime in the Leningrad Party (and, indeed, was to be quoted in the Indictment as going even further in conversation with relatives). Even though they may not have taken this seriously, merely listening to it could in retrospect be presented to them as complicity. In any case, mere close acquaintance with, or home proximity to, Nikolayev seems to have been enough to lead to arrest.

The only exception, and the only one apart from Nikolayev among all the eventual accused to have at least a measure of genuine guilt, was N. N. Shatsky.[7] He had been expelled from the Party in 1927. Though this expulsion was stated at the trial to have been for membership of the Zinoviev opposition, he seems, in fact, to have been a Trotskyite (and to have been an Anarchist at the time of the Revolution). Indeed, all true Zinovievites had applied for and received readmission to the Party, but he had never done so. A former worker, who became an engineer,[8] he had then suffered a good deal of petty persecution.[9] As with Nikolayev it was this that motivated him and not politics, which he seems to have given up.[10] He had come into contact with Nikolayev, and under the influence of the latter's ideas had actually taken to shadowing Kirov, with some notion of eventual action against him. Nikolayev did not, however, confide his own plans in him.[11] In the Indictment, while Nikolayev, Zvezdov, Antonov, Sokolov, and Yuskin are alleged to belong to one terrorist group, Shatsky is said to have had under his 'leadership' a group of his own, none of whose members are named.

But, as we have seen, Stalin soon took the decision to turn the case against the Zinovievites. Yezhov, visiting Moscow to receive further instructions, came back with this line fully developed;[12] and with Stalin's personally drafted list of the "Leningrad Terrorist Center's" membership.[13]

Nikolayev's acquaintances were an unimpressive lot. But this new move soon brought in more suitable victims.

The Leningrad Secret Political Department had naturally kept ex-Zinovievites on its files. In particular, it listed a number of former leaders of the Zinovievite Komsomol in Leningrad.[14] (The former Zinovievite leaders of the Leningrad Communist Party itself are all officially described as now living in Moscow.[15])

The ex-Zinovievites in Leningrad had indeed met together informally. The NKVD had long since suggested arresting the group's 'members', but Kirov had overruled them.[16] These were in fact precisely the men whom he had encouraged to work on the history of the Leningrad Komsomol. Indeed, in the Indictment of a later trial—that of August 1936 (see Chapter X)—it was stated that the Leningrad 'terrorists' had "enjoyed the confidence of a number of leading Party workers and officials of Soviet organisations in Leningrad."[17]

In their meetings, naturally enough, not everything said was in line with the official attitude; and Agranov was now able to use this to characterize them as 'illegal' meetings of the oppositionists.[18] The whole group, from whom six were finally selected for 'trial', seem to have been arrested on about 6 December.

Turning Nikolayev from an assassin with a personal grudge into a member of a political conspiracy presented certain problems to the interrogators.

Nikolayev had not been involved in the Zinoviev opposition. He had not been expelled or suspended from the Party during the struggle with that opposition, and had retained jobs in the ruling apparat. As we have seen, his only expulsion, and that not until March 1934, was simply for lack of discipline, in refusing an appointment; and even this was remitted in two months.

However, something could be made of this unpromising material. Anyone who had served in Leningrad in the early 1920s, and particularly as a member of the Komsomol, could be shown as contaminated. Nikolayev had been in the Vyborg district's branch, whose head was of course a Zinovievite—I. I. Kotolynov. And, though on one account Nikolayev had in fact been virulent against the Zinovievites, it is also said that he had more recently had some sort of contact with their history project, or at least that Shatsky had.[19]

Another difficulty arose with Nikolayev's diary and declarations, by now known in Leningrad NKVD and other circles. These, as we saw, made it clear that he had acted for personal reasons. However, suitable interrogation produced, on 13 December, an admission by Nikolayev of the "falsity and fictiousness" of these documents, which he had written "in order to conceal the participation of the Zinoviev group."[20] With "the object of masking the true motives for the murder of Comrade Kirov . . . this version was created in preliminary agreement with members of the terrorist group, who decided to represent the murder of Comrade Kirov as an individual act, and thereby to conceal the true motives of the crime."[21]

The six genuine ex-Zinovievites finally assembled for trial and another eight consisting mainly of Nikolayev and his friends were merged by the interrogators' skill into a single organization. It was divided for the purposes of the case into two categories. The 'Leningrad Terrorist Center' proper consisted of the Zinovievites plus Nikolayev and Shatsky (though at one point in the Indictment with a smaller membership, omitting the last two: in fact there were several variations given).[22]

In any case, Nikolayev's acquaintances were otherwise listed as not part of the "Center" but forming "terrorist groups" under its control. Only Kotolynov was both in the "Center" and leading such a group.[23]

The six genuine ex-Zinovievites were Kotolynov, V. V. Rumyantsev, S. O. Mandelstam, N. P. Myasnikov, V. S. Levin, and L. I. Sositsky. They had played important roles in the struggles of the 1920s—especially Rumyantsev and Kotolynov, then in their early twenties. (These two are described in the Indictment as the "principal" organizers of the conspiracy against Kirov).[24]

Rumyantsev had, as late as 1926, led the Leningrad Komsomol Committee in defeating a proposal to endorse the XIV Party Congress's condemnation of the Zinovievites.[25] Kotolynov, also a member of the Central Committee of the Komsomol, had strongly counterattacked the Stalinist element: "they have the mentality— 'if he is not a Stalinist, put on the screws, let him have it, chase him so hard that he won't open his mouth again.' "[26]

At the height of the struggle in 1926, Stalin's Komsomol chief A. V. Kosarev had been sent to Leningrad. Stalin perhaps brought him back to that city on his 1934 trip because it had already been tentatively decided to implicate the Kotolynov–Rumyantsev circle: a brief postponement to cope with the difficulties arising from Nikolayev's awkwardness being understandable.

Kosarev certainly had experience of this group. When the Leningrad Komsomol had continued its resistance and had refused to accept[27] the anti-Zinoviev decisions, Kosarev, as an envoy of the Center, could at first only get himself elected head of a Komsomol District Committee. But, as the months passed, he and his colleagues were able to bring the pressure of the central leadership to bear until local branches finally voted out their Zinovievite chiefs. This took much of 1926, in which year Kosarev represented the Leningrad Komsomol at the organization's Congress; and during that period he was engaged in bitter struggle against the leading Zinovievite Komsomols. He was thus the ideal man to finger the same men in the Kirov case. And when the Indictment was made public on 23 December, Kosarev's *Komsomolskaya Pravda* was the most detailed and violent in denunciation. "Kotolynov, Rumyantsev" and the others were "known in the Komsomol as capitulatory, unprincipled fractionists, base cowards, continual foul hangers-on of the Party, whining double-dealers, more than once deceiving the Party."[28]

And when the accused came to trial, it was plausibly alleged of them that their "organization possessed a number of links in places where the youth were concentrated."[29]

Meanwhile, behind the scenes, the case went forward. In the press, apart from the series of announcements of trials and executions of 'Whiteguards' and general appeals for relentless vigilance, nothing of what was afoot appeared.

There were newspaper articles on various themes such as the bestiality of fascism and (in *Pravda*) on "Crime in the United States."[30] A plenum of the Leningrad Provincial and City Committees on 15 December elected Zhdanov First Secretary, thus ending Chudov's temporary tenure;[31] and L. M. Zakovsky was appointed Head of the Leningrad NKVD. Presumably this meant that Agranov (and Mironov, if the latter had been covering the routine administration of the city's NKVD), returned to Moscow where, as we shall see, another investigation was pending. Zakovsky, who had joined the Secret Police at its very inception in 1918, was to prove himself one of the most ferocious and notorious of all the NKVD, and we shall come across him again in later chapters.

The case had by now matured to the point that (still for the moment secretly) Stalin felt able to proceed with the arrest, in Moscow, of the senior political figures of the Zinoviev group. On 16 December, though these arrests were not yet referred to, came the first direct public attack on Zinovievites as responsible for the murder. The Moscow Committee of the Party passed a resolution to the effect that "loathsome, hateful agents of the class enemy, foul dregs of the former Zinoviev antiparty group, have torn Comrade Kirov from our midst."[32]

And on 22 December, the NKVD announced that the investigation into Nikolayev and his accomplices had been concluded on 20 December. The act had been carried out on the orders of "the illegal terrorist 'Leningrad Center' " (described as "former members of the Zinoviev opposition"). Kotolynov, Rumyantsev, Mandelstam, Myasnikov, Levin, Sositsky, plus Nikolayev and Shatsky, with Sokolov, Zvezdov, Yuskin, Antonov, L. O. Khanik, and Tolmazov, were committed for trial before the Military Collegium. Kotolynov, Sokolov, Zvezdov, and Tolmazov are described as students; Shatsky as an engineer; the others as "employees." All the accused except Shatsky were members of the Communist Party at the time of their arrest.[33]

And the NKVD now announced the arrests, in Moscow, of the senior leaders of the old Zinovievite opposition,[34] which had in fact taken place some days ago.

After the murder, denunciations of the crime had been written by Zinoviev, then in the apparatus of the Trade Unions, by G. E. Evdokimov, then Head of the Milk Board, and by others. But these had not been published—and were later to be denounced as loathsome hypocrisy.[35]

Bakayev, Zinoviev's former Leningrad Secret Police Chief, and Evdokimov, Kirov's predecessor as Leningrad First Secretary and Secretary of the Central Committee, seem to have been arrested around 14 December.

Zinoviev drafted a letter to Yagoda saying he was disturbed by the arrests and asking to be summoned to establish that he "had nothing to do with this murder." He showed it to Kamenev, who seems to have dissuaded him from sending it.[36]

Zinoviev himself, with Kamenev and others, was arrested "in Moscow" on 16 December "in connection with" the Kirov murder.[37] Top NKVD officers came for them. K. V. Pauker, Head of the Operative Department, with P. P. Bulanov, Yagoda's personal assistant, arrested Kamenev; G. A. Molchanov, Head of the Secret Political Department, and A. I. Volovich (who was thus back in Moscow and no longer helping in Leningrad) took in Zinoviev.[38] There was no search of their apartments,[39] a presumable indication that no real suspicion of conspiracy existed.

Those now under arrest included Zinoviev himself, Kamenev, Evdokimov, Bakayev, G. F. Fedorov, G. I. Safarov, P. A. Zalutsky, A. S. Kuklin, L. Y. Faivilovich, N. V. Vardin, I. S. Gorshenin, V. S. Bulakh, A. M. Gertik, Y. V. Sharov, and A. P. Kostina—believed to be Bakayev's wife.[40] (Apart from Zinoviev and Evdokimov, the less prominent figures Zalutsky, Kuklin, Bakayev, and Safarov are elsewhere named as prominent in the old Leningrad machine. and so presumably living in more or less a condition of exile in Moscow.[41])

Zinoviev and Kamenev (both former members of the Polit-

buro), Evdokimov (former secretary of the Central Committee),
Zalutsky, Kuklin, Fedorov, and Safarov were all former members
of the Central Committee.

The announcement was, up to a point, inconclusive. It stated
that the the cases of Zinoviev himself, Kamenev, Evdokimov,
Fedorov, Zalutsky, Safarov, and Vardin, "in connection with
whom the investigation has established that sufficient material for
their committal to trial is absent, have been handed over for examination to the Special Board of the NKVD with a view to the summary exile of these persons. Investigations in connection with the
other arrested persons are proceeding."[42] (The Special Board of
the NKVD was one of the new Stalinist bodies, empowered at this
point only to sentence, without trial, up to five years imprisonment.)

Zinoviev, Kamenev, and others in fact came to trial, as we shall
see, the following month. Meanwhile, the 'Leningrad Center' trial
went forward.

On 25 December the Indictment of the Leningrad Center was
drawn up, and published the following day.[43] As we have said, the
plotters were divided into two groups. Kotolynov is the sole Zinovievite named in the group he supposedly headed, though he provided the link to the 'Center', of which he was a member; and his
'group' included Nikolayev and all the non-Center rank-and-file of
the alleged plot except Shatsky; the other group "under the leadership of N. N. Shatsky" had no specified membership.

The only man not named specifically as a member of either one
of the groups or of the Center is L. O. Khanik. He may have been
a more or less accidental victim. His elder brother Mikhail was an
important engineer in the legendary Putilov Works, under the cele-
brated M. K. Ots, one of Kirov's closest collaborators in the industrial field; and Mikhail Khanik himself, as we have seen, seems
also to have enjoyed Kirov's protection. He had indeed been a
Zinovievite, and retained acquaintance with the members of the
'Center'. The elder Khanik had succeeded in committting suicide
and his brother was arrested more or less as a substitute.[44] The
Khaniks' sister is reported as drowning herself, and the mother was
sent to a psychiatric clinic.[45]

It was noted that "In the interests of secrecy, the members of the Center met together very rarely."[46] The animus was not merely Zinovievite—the accused are also quoted as speaking of the "Trotsky–Zinoviev bloc." "One of the members" of the group (unnamed) had the "complete files of the Trotsky–Zinoviev opposition" which were "seized" by the NKVD—though not published or entered in evidence: nor did they ever appear.[47] The contact with Trotsky was maintained through the "—Consul in Leningrad, who also provided 5,000 rubles. Nikolayev also "supplied information on certain questions which interested the consul."[48] This referred to the Latvian Consul George Bissenieks, a Social Democrat (facilitating the Trotsky connection). As we have noted, Nikolayev's Latvian wife had indeed known the consul,[49] and Nikolayev is reported as having met him, so that this was a comparatively veridical charge. It was not to be pursued beyond this point.

The Indictment also specifically attacks the "émigré Whiteguard, landlord and capitalist organizations, 'the Russian General Military League' and the 'Fraternity of Russian Truth' (Denikinists)—who openly advocate terrorism and systematically smuggle their agents on to the territory of the USSR with the object of organizing and perpetrating terrorist acts against representatives of the Soviet government."[50] Thus some sort of a link, though without any particular evidence, is established with the already executed 'Whiteguards.'

The Indictment mentions evidence taken from Nikolayev's wife, Milda Draule, and his mother M. T. Nikolayeva. Of these two, it only quotes the former, who says that Nikolayev had refused to take a job since the end of March 1934. She "presumed" the reason he did so was in order not "to be tied," having "dedicated himself completely to the preparation of this terrorist act."[51] His brother Petr is quoted, more substantially, as telling the interrogators "Leonid also told me that the overthrow of the Soviet government was possible only as a result of an attack by foreign capitalist states and that, if he were abroad, he would help in every way any capitalist state that would attack the Soviet Union in order to overthrow the Soviet government."[52]

Another unidentified 'relative' of Nikolayev, R. M. Kulishev, testified that the assassin had said to him that "intervention against the Soviet Union was to be expected in the near future" and that he deduced that Nikolayev "would be pleased if intervention actually took place."[53] Though much is made of this family evidence in the Indictment, none of it directly implicated Nikolayev in any plot. But, if even partly true, it implies that he was talking imprudently.

Only Nikolayev and two of his acquaintances, Zvezdov and Antonov, are stated in the Indictment as having "fully admitted" their guilt.[54] Shatsky simply "did not admit his guilt." Rumyantsev, Levin, Myasnikov, Tolmazov, and Khanik only admitted membership of the 'group', as did Mandelstam, who specifically "denied knowledge of the terrorist methods of operation of this group." Sositsky admitted membership, and awareness of the "terrorist sentiments" of the group. Kotolynov admitted membership of the group, denied "direct participation in the assassination" but admitted that as a member and leader of the group he bore "responsibility for the crime." Sokolov also admitted membership, but denied direct participation, while Yuskin denied membership but admitted knowing of the preparation for the killing.[55]

The Indictment was drawn up in Leningrad and signed by the already notorious Vyshinsky and by L. Sheinin, the Procuratorship's "Investigator of Important Cases," and countersigned by the USSR Procurator A. I. Akulov.[56]

The trial took place in camera on 28–29 December 1934, with Ulrich, Matulevich, and Goryachev as judges. It was at once obvious that a public trial would have been a failure.

There are several accounts of what happened. Those present were largely NKVD personnel (some of them there to gain experience) together, reportedly, with a number of others under arrest and not now on trial. On one account, Nikolayev was kept behind a screen apart from the others.[57]

The secretary of the court, Military Jurist First Rank A. A. Batner, who had actually handed Nikolayev the indictment, later said that he was the only one to plead guilty and incriminate the others. Nikolayev, he added, behaved calmly and spoke a great deal in court.[58] He had, it appears, been promised his life through his investigator Katsafa, and when he heard his sentence to death, he became angry and repentant at having implicated the others.[59] The others continued to insist on their innocence.

Levin, though frequently interrupted by the judge, made a stout speech attacking the party leadership as well as defending his own innocence. When he started to speak of Stalin, he was hustled from the court.[60] They were all found guilty and sentenced to death. They were shot that night in the Liteyni Prison cellars.[61] Kotolynov is reported as denouncing the case with his last breath.[62]

In many ways the Indictment and the report of the 'trial' are clumsy documents. But even the great set-piece trials of 1936–1938, which took months of careful preparation, had their mistakes and inconsistencies, and the team working on the Leningrad Center only had a few weeks.

Still, not only the public, but also the Party—and the world— knew nothing of what was going on in the investigation or, apart from a brief official announcement, at the trial. For them, generally speaking, the Zinovievite plot was perfectly plausible. In fact, in a milieu where everything had become political, such a scenario was more credible than that of a lone assassin. Even Trotsky— though at once noting that Stalin and Yagoda rather than Zinoviev and Kamenev were behind it—took it for granted that a group of young dissidents had carried out the actual murder.[63]

CHAPTER VIII

The Second Story:
The 'Moscow Center'

The cases of Zinoviev, Kamenev, and others had been dropped for lack of evidence on 20 December.

On 16 January 1935, however, it was announced that "the investigation in the case of I. P. Bakayev, A. M. Gertik, A. S. Kuklin, and others"—those sent for further investigation on 20 December—had produced "new material relating to the underground counterrevolutionary activities of G. E. Zinoviev, G. E. Evdokimov, L. B. Kamenev, and G. F. Fedorov."[1]

It is notable that hardly a word of this had come out at the Nikolayev trial only a fortnight earlier. In the Indictment of that case made out on 25 December, there was no allegation of any involvement by Zinoviev and the others; no connection with any 'Moscow Center'; and, on Zinoviev's political responsibility, only the vague statement that the 'Leningrad Center' was based "on the platform of the Trotsky–Zinoviev bloc, which aimed at undermining the authority of the existing Party leadership and securing its replacement by the leaders of the organization—Zinoviev, Kamenev, and the others, who are in favor of changing the line now pursued by the Party."[2] And from that trial itself on 28–29 December there was also only the statement that the group had undertaken terrorism with the aim of "achieving a change in present policy in the spirit of the so-called Zinoviev–Trotsky platform."[3]

The only date we have for testimony from the new interrogation quoted from the Moscow accused is that of Bakayev, on 4 January 1935. Bakayev, who is named (with Safarov) as the main source of testimony against the accused, was among those earliest arrested and is reported as treated with some harshness. It appears that his may have been the earliest usable testimony.[4] At any rate, these allegations of "underground counterrevolutionary activities" against the accused had not been possible on 28 December but had become so a week later.

Pressure was now put on Zinoviev and the others.

Zinoviev and Kamenev had twice already been expelled from the Party and publicly repented. Each time they had been readmitted. Each time the repentance had been more abject. The differencc now was that it was required before a court—not, from a Party point of view, more than a step further. And they seem, or so both official and unofficial reports tell us, to have nourished the hope not only that they would once again be rehabilitated, but eventually be recalled to the leadership from which they had only been excluded for nine years—a prospect that would perhaps have had some semblance of probability in a Kirov-type regime, though hardly likely as long as Stalin retained his current ascendancy.

The Indictment, drawn up on 13 January, based its charges on an alleged 'Zinoviev–Trotsky platform'. The "underground counterrevolutionary 'Moscow Center' " proper consisted of Zinoviev, Kamenev, Evdokimov, Bakayev, Kuklin, Fedorov, Gertik, I. S. Gorshenin, and Y. V. Sharov.[5] L. Y. Faivilovich was also listed. And there were nine new accused: I. I. Tarasov, N. A. Tsarkov, B. L. Bravo, A. V. Herzberg, S. M. Hessen, B. N. Sakhov, A. F. Bashkirov, A. V. Perimov, and A. L. Anishev.[6]

All the accused had been expelled from the Party in 1927 (and reinstated in 1928–1929 on declaring their "complete solidarity with the policy of the Party and the Government") except for Gorshenin, Herzberg, and Sakhov (the last of whom had, however, received a 'severe reprimand and warning on factional activities').[7] Zinoviev and Kamenev, but none of the others, had again been expelled in 1932 for reading and not reporting the

'Ryutin Platform', but once more reinstated in 1933. (With the
lesser figures there was the occasional slip up in the Indictment:[8]
for example, Anishev is described as a member of the "Moscow
counterrevolutionary underground group" early in the Indictment,
and of the "Leningrad underground counterrevolutionary Zinoviev
group" later.)[9]

At first the 'chief' leaders—Zinoviev, Kamenev, and Gertik—
had made 'disavowals' in the investigation, but the other accused
had incriminated them.[10] And except for Kamenev, all the accused
had finally confessed at the investigation to active membership
of the 'Center', or of the 'counterrevolutionary Zinoviev group'
(with four of them—Tsarkov, Bashkirov, Tarasov, and Anishev—
members of 'the *Leningrad* underground counterrevolutionary Zinoviev group').[11]

Zinoviev "admitted his guilt," confirming the existence of the
Center and his own participation in the Center. Kamenev is quoted
has having "admitted his guilt," but only confessing to counterrevolutionary activities and membership of the Moscow Center up
to 1932, retaining later connections with Zinoviev "only because
of personal reasons," though he had not counteracted the oppositionists' degeneration "actively and energetically" enough.[12]

One of the accused, Fedorov, admitted that "the members of
the organization were disseminators of the most abominable slan-
ders, rumors and gossip regarding the leadership of the Party,"
saying also that "the organization stopped at nothing in the dis-
semination of calumnies and lies, deception and distorted facts, in
other words they resorted to the most abominable methods bor-
rowed from the arsenal of fascism."[13] In still other words, they
said things about the Stalinists which the Stalinists would have
preferred not to have had recounted.

Though Zinoviev and Kamenev had submitted to the Party line,
and were conducting no anti-Party political activity, they had
surely spoken in their own circle, we can assume, in terms other
than those of orthodox adulation of Stalinism, and had passed on
more or less malicious intra-Party gossip.

When it came to terrorism—since no access to the accused, or
public trial, had been allowed in the Nikolayev–Kotolynov case—
it may be that even Zinoviev and his friends thought that some, at

least, of their former young Leningrad supporters had carried out
the murder; or, at any rate, that Nikolayev might in some sense
have acted on the principles of opposition which they had once
circulated.

Even if they were skeptical about the political affiliations of Nikolayev (as perhaps they were not), they might find it hard to re-
but (even in their own minds) the notion that anything less than
a total repudiation and disavowal of notions hostile to the Party
line might leave such assassins taking encouragement, or even incitement, from the idea of their opposition.

At any rate, over the period since their arrest, it had been put
to them that they must once again 'disarm'. As we have noted, Zinoviev and Kamenev had already done so twice—in 1928, when
they repented for their earlier opposition; and again in 1933, after
their brief second expulsion.

Once again, they were told that the Party needed the repudiation of any tinge of opposition, the expression of total loyalty to
the Stalin leadership, and the acceptance of the charge that, however indirectly, their stance might have encouraged the assassination.

The Indictment maintained that the Moscow Center had "acted
as a political center, which for a number of years systematically
guided the underground counterrevolutionary activities both of the
Moscow and the Leningrad groups."[14]

Visits to Leningrad by Kuklin, Gertik, Evdokimov, and Sharov
had "maintained counterrevolutionary contacts with the members
of the Leningrad Center."[15] There seems no special reason to
doubt that some of the senior Zinovievites had, from time to time,
met their former subordinates in Leningrad. Bakayev was accused
of having been on good terms with Levin,[16] (though even in his
final total confession in 1936 Bakayev said that their meeting was
not for terrorist purposes[17]), and apparently Zinoviev had met
him in 1932.[18]

Levin and others of the Leningrad group were quoted as having
confessed that they had been 'empowered' by the Moscow Center.
Bakayev, Evdokimov, Gorshenin, Fedorov, and Sharov had 'cor-
roborated' this, as had Bravo, Anishev, and Hessen—and Safarov

(who was not among the accused, his case having been 'set aside for further examination').[19]

In his evidence at the investigation, Zinoviev is quoted as saying that his earlier anti-Party struggle "could not but have contributed to the degeneration of these miscreants" and that the Party was "absolutely right" about "the political responsibility of the former anti-Party 'Zinoviev' group for the assassination."[20]

The investigation had nevertheless "not established facts which might serve as grounds for directly accusing the members of the 'Moscow Center' of having given their consent to, or of having given instructions for the organization of the terrorist act against Comrade Kirov." But the whole "atmosphere" and "character" of their activities "prove that they were aware of the terrorist sentiments of the members of the group and that they inflamed those sentiments," a phrase repeated in the sentence.[21]

The report of the investigation concluded, "And thus the members of the 'Moscow Center' and particularly the accused Zinoviev, Evdokimov, Gertik and Kamenev, must bear not only moral and political responsibility, but also responsibility before Soviet law for the consequence of their underground activities which induced their Leningrad group to resort to terrorists acts."[22]

The trial took place in Leningrad, and was in camera. The actual trial was skimpily covered. *Pravda* printed a summary as follows:

> The accused confessed that they tried to safeguard their cadres, to accumulate power, and to strengthen their supporters' feelings of bitterness and open hatred for the leaders of the Party and for Soviet power.
>
> They confessed that double-dealing, fraud, and treachery constituted the characteristic tricks of struggle adopted and widely practiced by the participants in the counterrevolutionary underground, Zinovievist group.
>
> They confessed that in their struggle against the Party and Government they did not shrink from employing "the foulest means borrowed from fascism's arsenal."
>
> They confessed that all of their "thoughts and ideas led to the

staging of a bourgeois-restorationist reaction against socialism."
They confessed that "all counterrevolutionary, anti-Party group-
ings were amalgamated into one solid mass in their anti-Party
underground."

They confessed that they "became the activators of the counterrevolutionary malice and anger of the remnants of the exploiting
classes" against the dictatorship of the proletariat. And, finally,
they were forced by the weight of the evidence to confess that in
that poisonous, Zinovievist underground counterrevolutionary
cesspool they developed and strengthened authentic Whiteguard
methods of struggle against Soivet power, and an openly terroristic temperament that led to the foul murder of Comrade
Kirov.[23]

Apart from this rather general and doubtless prejudiced summary,
there was almost no reporting of the trial, apart from excerpts
from Evdokimov's "declaration," presumably the most acceptable.
Pravda published these at length. Evdokimov (it said) declared:
"I made a great error at the beginning of the investigation, as did
Zinoviev and a number of others." This particular "error" had
consisted in claiming that they had, in fact, become reconciled, if
not to the Stalin ascendancy as such, at least to the Party line. For
they had erred "in saying that in our counterrevolutionary attitudes there were periods in which these attitudes softened. This
was not really so, and our counterrevolutionary convictions remained the same, and active to the last."

He condemned their "malicious counterrevolutionary insinua-
tions against Comrade Stalin." He said that Zinoviev and Kamenev
had deceived the XVII Congress with their protestations. He rejected a plea of Zinoviev's that "subjectively" they had remained
loyal to the working class, saying that both subjectively and objectively they had betrayed.

Evdokimov spoke of the group's "bad relations with the Party
leadership," said that the group had opposed collectivization and
industrialization, and had accused the leadership of slowing down
the development of the international working-class movement, citing an opinion of Zinoviev's in late 1934 that the "initiative and
leadership of the workers' movement in France had been surrend-
ered to the Second International."

They had (Evdokimov continued) welcomed rumors of disputes in the Central Committee, which had raised their hopes. Perhaps an oblique reference to Kirov.

On the Kirov murder itself he confessed—"When we are blamed for a terrorist attitude, I firmly declare: yes, for that we must take responsibility, for the venom by which we poisoned those who surrounded us over the last decade and which made possible a supreme crime, the murder of Kirov."

He also made it clear that the leading accused had definitely asserted that no 'Moscow Center' activity had taken place for some time: "It is known to me from the material of the preliminary investigation that some of the defendants consider that the activation of the Zinovievist organization's Leningrad Center allegedly coincided with the passivity of action of the Moscow Center. That wasn't so, but even if it were, what meaning does it have? The venom continued to work. All of our accomplices throught that we stood for our previous positions, and that we stood for them actively." Evdokimov ended with a warm tribute to "the Party's leader of genius, Comrade Stalin."[24]

Apart from Evdokimov's, the accused's testimony at the trial itself was given very meagerly at the time; but at their later trial in 1936 it was quoted at greater length. By that time, the prosecution had a different purpose: to show that Zinoviev and the others had in January 1935 *not,* in fact, confessed properly when they should have done. So we learn that Kamenev had actually said then that he had always found the witness Safarov quite untrustworthy, and that he did not know of the existence of the Moscow Center, of which he seemed to be a member, though insofar as it existed he would take responsibility for it.[25] As for Zinoviev, he maintained that many in the dock were unknown to him,[26] and that he had learned of Kotolynov's role only from the published Indictment of the 'Leningrad Center' case.[27] Even Evdokimov is then quoted as denying any connection with the Kirov murder.[28]

It is clear from this that what actually occurred at the trial is notably different from what was reported. The conclusion seems to be that Zinoviev and Kamenev did indeed 'disarm' politically, but that they made important denials of many of the allegations published as proved and admitted in the Soviet press in January 1935.

The 'Whiteguard' line was also now heavily stressed, though again without allegations of direct links. *Pravda* even referred to "the Zinovievite–Whiteguard groups in Moscow and Leningrad," together with general allegations of their "sinking in to complete Whiteguardery," and of their having won the applause "only of the counterrevolutionary bourgeois Whiteguard emigrants and fascists." In the *Pravda* 'summing up' of the evidence there is a reference to "Whiteguard methods of struggle."[29]

The papers printed calls from stormy factory meetings throughout the USSR demanding the shooting of the accused.[30] But the time was not yet ripe, and Stalin himself is reported as proposing in the Politburo that execution should not be resorted to.[31]

Ulrikh, Matulevich, and Goryachev, again constituting the Military Collegium of the Supreme Court, sentenced Zinoviev, Gertik, Kuklin, and Sakhov to ten years imprisonment, as the "active leaders" and "most active members" of the underground group; they sentenced most of the others to eight or six years for "active participation" and "membership"; and they imposed only five years each on Kamenev, Bashkirov, and Bravo as "less active members." Those sentenced were sent to the "political isolators" at Verkhne Uralsk and Chelyabinsk, where conditions for political prisoners were at this time still quite tolerable. But a few years later none survived.

We know little of the fate of their relatives: Antonov-Ovseenko relates that Fedorov's wife Beta spent eighteen years in labor camp, and that their five daughters also went to NKVD centers; and no doubt the fate of other families was no better.

At the same time as the announcement of the Moscow Center verdict, a statement of the NKVD was issued to the effect that an NKVD Special Board, with its overtly nonjudicial procedures, "adopted a decision in the case of members of the counterrevolutionary Zinoviev group." Seventy-eight people were sentenced to camp or exile.[32]

Among the forty-nine sentenced to "confinement in concentration camps for a period of four to five years" were former Central Committee member P. A. Zalutsky, V. S. Bulakh, and A. P. Kostina, all of whom had been on the original, 16 December list of those arrested and to be investigated. There were also a number of identifiable Zinovievites of the second rank, such as G. I. Mironov, a Leningrad delegate to the XIV Party Congress in 1925. And some of the others appear to be wives or relatives of the accused, including a sister and a half-sister of Nikolayev's.

Twenty-nine others of the 'group' were sentenced to be exiled to various points for a period of two to five years." Fewer of these are identifiable, though we find Yuskin's wife, A. Y. Yuskina, and Nikolayev's mother, M. T. Nikolayeva and his sister-in-law, A. A. Nikolayeva-Maximova.[33] The last on this list was G. I. Safarov, arrested with the leaders in mid-December. He had been the most compliant 'witness' in the recent case and seems to have survived imprisonment longer than his colleagues, dying only in 1943.[34]

Not all those involved in the case were on these lists. Nikolayev's wife Milda and brother Petr seem already to have been sentenced.[35] We are told that all the 'witnesses' at the Nikolayev trial were in fact shot;[36] and that Borisov's wife, after being sent to psychiatric hospital and escaping, was liquidated more unofficially.[37] Many others were arrested and sentenced without public announcement.

By March, estimates of Leningrad arrests and deportations ran at 60,000 to 100,000: including, in particular, members of the dispossessed classes; 4,000 families were exiled to Astrakhan alone.[38] This massive operation was noted by the American Embassy, while the British Ambassador Lord Chilton reported that it was owing to the presence of those prerevolutionary strata that only in Leningrad had there still been "any trace of public opinion," which the current purge was aimed at settling for good and all.[39]

But no class was exempt. The Leningrad prisons—the Shpalerny, the Kresti, the Nizhegorodsky—were full; and inmates included a wide selection: many older workers from the factories, students, engineers from the Higher Technical School.[40] Two men, workers from the Marty shipyard, were jailed for running away from the procession which accompanied Kirov's body to the train, and "inciting" others to do likewise. They got three years.[41]

A Leningrad area peasant in the Kresti Prison early in 1935 had had the following conversation. A stranger had said to him:

"Have you heard that Kirov has been killed"?

"Its all the same to me," answered Ivan, who had no idea who Kirov was, "Every day some one gets killed. Today its your Kirov, tomorrow its someone else."

The stranger called the police, and the peasant found himself charged with incitement to kill Stalin. However, he only got ten years.[42]

More immediately, and more menacing, the trial was followed up, on 18 January 1935, by a confidential Central Committee circular to all Party organizations calling for a full-scale rooting out of enemies of the people.[43]

CHAPTER IX

The Police Connection

On 23 January 1935 the police officials whose arrest had been announced on 4 December were brought to trial. We noted the surprising omission of Zaporozhets's name among those originally blamed. This was now remedied. It is said that Voroshilov noticed the omission and drew attention to it (which seems to show that Voroshilov, at least, was in no way privy to the affair).[1] In any case, Zaporozhets (and three others previously unnamed, A. M. Belousenko, M. I. Kotomin, and A. A. Gubin) were now brought before the Military Collegium of the Supreme Court under, as ever, Ulrikh, this time joined by Matulevich and Golyakov.

On the basis of "investigation" and "the confession of the accused," it was established that the accused "and especially M. S. Bal'tsevich," had "had at their disposal information about the preparations for the assassination of Comrade Kirov, and yet had shown not merely carelessness, but criminal negligence in regard to the basic requirements of the defense of state security and had not taken the necessary measures."

Medved, Zaporozhets, and Gorin-Ludrin had "failed to take measures to discover and end in good time the activity of the terrorist Zinovievite group in Leningrad, among them the assassin of Comrade Kirov, the villainous Nikolayev, even though they had every opportunity to do so."

All had, *Pravda* said, pleaded guilty. Medved and Zaporozhets were sentenced to three years for "criminal negligence in official duty concerning State security"; and Gubin, Kotomin, and Petrov also each received three years for "criminal negligence in their official duty." Fomin, Gorin-Ludrin, Yanishevsky, Mosevich, Belousenko, and Lobov each got two years, for "negligence in their official duty." And Bal'tsevich got ten years "for criminal negligence in his official duty of defending State security, and for a number of illegal actions during the investigation."[2]

Bal'tsevich's particular criminal negligence, if he was in charge of security arrangements at the Smolny, is clear enough. The absence of guards had been remarked by Chudov and all the others who came out into the third-floor corridor after the fatal shot. It was the only suspicious point that they ventured even to mention to Stalin.[3] A heavy sentence would seem indicated for this reason alone. What is not clear is what the charge of "illegal actions during the investigation" might signify. It must refer to something that took place over the night of 1 December and the early morning of 2 December before the Moscow team took over. Which is to say that it most probably refers to the interrogation of Nikolayev himself.

It is plausible to consider that, in Zaporozhets's absence, Bal'tsevich was the leading member of his conspiracy present in Leningrad. As we have noted, accounts agree that by the time Stalin arrived Nikolayev had somehow become aware that the NKVD had been using him.[4] Yet in the absence of Zaporozhets[5] it must not have been Zaporozhets himself, but an officer in his confidence who had made the original contacts with Nikolayev, and who had committed the unnecessary blunder of in one way or another alerting Nikolayev to the fact. (He could, of course, be charged with having "falsely" suggested the NKVD involvement to Nikolayev.)

The Indictment speaks of Bal'tsevich's illegal "actions." Another might be that Bal'tsevich was responsible for putting Nikolayev's diary into the record before it could be suppressed. This must have been before the murder of Borisov, since the Moscow NKVD men were by then in charge. But it is also conceivable that Bal'tsevich in some way mishandled Borisov, who was still available, not getting killed until the Moscow men were in control: he would, moreover, be a member of Bal'tsevich's Operative Department of security guards. This is all speculation; but it is speculation within a fairly limited range of possibilities.

Indeed, while the Moscow Center case made the most of what were largely imponderables, the police trial revealed very little about what were, even on the most favorable reckoning, important facts. Apart from Bal'tsevich's, the most obvious oddity in the sentences was, of course, their mildness. In particular, that "criminal negligence" warranted only three years as against two years for ordinary "negligence" is on the face of it incomprehensible.

Among Leningrad's police and party leaders, it must have indeed been clear by the time Stalin and Agranov arrived on 2 December that there was something fishy about the murder. Rumors reached the diplomatic corps, as early as December, that the NKVD were involved.[6]

Trotsky's belief in Stalin's responsibility was argued as follows. If the Leningrad NKVD leadership knew of the plan to assassinate Kirov, and let it go ahead, it could hardly have been on their own initiative. Their chiefs must have reported regularly to Yagoda in Moscow. And Yagoda would not have allowed such an operation without Stalin's approval, or on his suggestion. The logic is reasonable: but it still remained to be proved. Trotsky held that the plan was to thwart the attempt at the last moment, and still use it against the Zinovievites. And junior officers involved in the plot are indeed said to have been told that the NKVD meant to prevent the assassination at the last moment, and that it was only intended as a demonstration of the dangers still lurking among the population.[7]

But it was the shortness of the sentences which first produced a conviction about the affair in police circles outside Leningrad that there was more to the matter than mere negligence. As one of them commented, "genuine negligence on the part of the NKVD officers in preventing assassination, of which [Stalin] himself was an obvious potential target, would inevitably have resulted in the summary execution of all concerned."[8]

There was no open attempt to justify the short sentences. But, more informally, it was allowed to be known that the NKVD officers allegedly pled in court that, though guilty, they were only so because they had acted on Kirov's own instructions.[9] This could of course be supported by proving that they had indeed discovered, and reported to Kirov on, the Kotolynov circle, and been instructed to leave them alone. As to the inadequacy of the guard arrangements, that too—if less plausibly—could be blamed on a lax attitude to security on Kirov's part, perhaps eked out (as was done later) with putting some of the blame on Borisov. In the Secretariat of the Leningrad NKVD, the view put about was that Kirov had been against an adequate guard, and was impatient when Chekists escorted him. Thus they "held responsible for the tragic loss, the disgraceful carelessness and inadequate class vigilance of Kirov himself."[10] According to one story circulating in the Leningrad NKVD, Kirov himself had ordered Nikolayev's release on one suspicious occasion.[11] A former Smolny official too, later jailed but released and rehabilitated in 1958, said they were told not only that Kirov had been Milda Nikolayeva's lover, but also that he had personally had Nikolayev released after his first arrest at the Smolny.[12]

But even this failed to convince veteran officers that the light sentences were natural to the occasion.

This suspicion became even stronger when it became known how the sentences were in fact served. These had been spcifically to "imprisonment in concentration camp." And, formally speaking, this turned out to be true.

Yagoda who had treated them with "exceptional and unusual solicitude" throughout their arrest and trial, saw Medved and Zaporozhets before they left, and entrusted the care of their families to his Secretary, Bulanov. They were sent to camp in "a special railroad car" and not in a prison wagon.[13]

The "exceptional solicitude" shown by Yagoda was matched by that of his subordinates. Contrary to the whole Stalinist tradition of breaking instantly with anyone in disgrace, Pauker, the Head of the NKVD Operative Department (and of Stalin's bodyguard), and Shanin, (Head of the NKVD Transport Department), were, a colleague noted, sending Zaporozhets's gramophone records and a radio—Shanin saying how much he sympathized with Zaporozhets's position.[14]

Medved was sent first to Medvezhaya Gora, headquarters of the White Sea Canal camps, arriving by train in a private compartment and being put up by the head of the project, Rappaport, in his own home, where he even gave a party for him. Medved wore an NKVD uniform without the insignia of his rank, (and he and his Leningrad colleagues are henceforth spoken of by all witnesses as dressed in this fashion). He went on, in the same style, to the Solovki camps on the White Sea.[15]

This doubtless happened in the early months of 1935, before the ice of the Okhotsk Sea melted sufficiently for him and his colleagues to be sent to their final destination, the gold-mining camp complex of Kolyma.

Kolyma was a good choice for an area of exile. Wholly under the control of the NKVD, the furthest of the great 'islands' of the Gulag Archipelago was also the most isolated. It was then only accessible by boat from Vladivostok or one of the nearby ports, to Nagayevo, just south of its capital, Magadan. The present writer has described the area, and given its history, in *Kolyma: The Arctic Death Camps*.

It was by no means the White Hell it later became. The climate is extremely cold, but very healthy for people who are properly fed and clothed. There had been enormous casualties while the gold camps were being established in 1931–1933; but by 1935 it was well administered and, as far as even the prisoners were concerned, one of the best areas to be in. The rational consideration that the production of gold was so important to the economy that the miners needed to be in good condition still prevailed. It was only at the end of 1937 that warm clothes were withdrawn, minimal ration scales introduced, and impossible schedules fixed, with the evident intention, and the actual result, that the very word "Kolyma" is still one of horror in the Soviet mind, as the place where millions later died of cold, hunger, and execution.

An NKVD officer serving in the area describes the arrival of Medved and Zaporozhets on the official passenger steamer *Soviet* (unlike the many fearful tales of prisoners who came on the true slave ships, *Nikolai Yezhov, Dzhurma, Dalstroy,* and the others). This was in May 1935, the earliest time at which the icebreaker *Krassin* could bring the ships in. A sister of one of them is reported with them. They had two carloads of baggage. Wearing their uniforms, without badges or rank as before, they were put up in the Magadan hotel, with a table to themselves in the hotel restaurant.

They were well treated by E. Berzin, the Head of Dalstroy, and given "assistant" posts in their various new responsibilities—which were the top positions in reality, and were soon made so in practice.[16]

In addition to Medved and Zaporozhets, Fomin, Yanishevsky, Mosevich, and Gubin (and, apparently, Lobov) are reported in Kolyma by various sources,[17] and it seems plausible that others of the Leningrad contingent also served there.

On one account Medved was eventually offered the job of head of the Records and Assignments division of Dalstroy,[18] but refused it on the grounds of his responsibility for the Kirov case, becoming a common prisoner, but keeping his Party card; but, if so, this was only an interlude. His wife was allowed to join him, which would hardly have been possible for a worker; though she eventually returned.[19] Medved is certainly described by a more junior NKVD officer, who worked with him in Kolyma, as a devoted adherent of the principle that sacrifices such as his were necessary for the eventual triumph of world Communism—and all the usual Stalinist line. But this subordinate saw him in his office in his own three-room house. He drank a lot and seemed a little crazed. He only once referred to the Kirov affair. He then told his junior that in a personal interview Stalin himself had said to him that he had committed a grave offense: he had failed to protect the life of Kirov. This was "inexcusable." But, considering his earlier service to the Party, Stalin hoped in three years time to be able to use his services again. "I know Stalin himself fairly well; I know how all this happened," Medved remarked, adding, "I know well how Kirov was killed, by whom, and why."[20]

Medved never returned to the subject.

This was perhaps when Medved is reported as heading the Kolyma Transport Administration, and Fomin ran the NKVD

"Special Sections" of Kolyma;[21] but sometime during 1935–1937 the appointments may have changed. Fomin and Zaporozhets are later definitely named as heading the Kolyma Road-Building Administration, in Yagodnoye.[22] A. A. Mosevich is identified as Head of the NKVD Secret Political Department of Dalstroy;[23] while Gubin was Head of the Shturmovoy mine complex, and Yanishevsky of the Berzin (later called Upper At-Urakh) mine complex.[24] These two were large enterprises employing 12,000 to 15,000 prisoners, and are within twenty or thirty miles of each other, and of Yagodnoye where Zaporozhets and Fomin worked, all in the Northern Administration of the Kolyma gold camps.

Yanishevsky, whose wife (like Medved's) was allowed to join him after six months,[25] told an acquaintance that while he was absolutely barred from telling what had really happened in the Kirov case, he would say that at any rate it was quite different from what had been reported in the press.[26]

This extraordinary treatment of men who were, on the face of it, convicted prisoners, became widely known. The "Letter of an Old Bolshevik" (1936) already knew that the police officials had been "given responsible positions in the administration" of the camps to which they were sent.[27]

What was not discussable, even in the high NKVD circles which more or less openly protected and comforted Zaporozhets and the others, was the true essence of the case. Two high Foreign Department operatives, when in Moscow, were each told by home-based colleagues that (in the words of one of them) "the whole affair is so dangerous that it is healthier not to know too much about it."[28]

As we have seen, Yanishevsky and Medved felt constrained to keep their counsels, though their hints, if reported, may have been thought excessive. At any rate, as Khrushchev put it, "in 1937 they were shot. We can assume that they were shot in order to cover up the traces of the organizers of Kirov's killing."[29] Lobov, Head of the Leningrad Secret Political Department, was among those executed.[30]

But this purge took place late in the year, probably in December 1937, in any case long after Yagoda's arrest in early April, so it was not a matter of protecting *him*. Berzin, their boss in

Kolyma, was arrested then, together with almost all his camp chiefs and other subordinates, in whose alleged plots the Leningraders, too, might readily have been implicated. Their families, as was customary, would have been involved, though we only know of Medved's schoolboy son, Misha, who got a five-year sentence as "member of the family of an enemy of the people."[31]

It is curious to note that in the 1936 trial of the 'Trotskyite–Zinovievite Terrorist Center' (see the next chapter), Vyshinsky alleged in his closing speech for the prosecution that Zinoviev and Kamenev had intended Bakayev to be Chairman of the OGPU if they succeeded in seizing power. Bakayev would then liquidate "the traces of their foul crimes" by destroying "the very people who had carried out Zinoviev and Kamenev's instructions." Zinoviev and Kamenev, Vyshinsky said, had admitted the plan to appoint Bakayev, but had denied the rest as "fantastic tales from the Arabian Nights," or (in Zinoviev's words) taken "from Jules Verne." Yet, Vyshinsky had insisted, the allegation was true.[32]

Two Leningraders, Fomin and Petrov, survived. Petrov had been in charge of matters concerned with the Leningrad military and was thus perhaps deputy head of the Special Department. Fomin was eventually released and evidently rehabilitated, but refused to discuss the Kirov case even then.[33] Unless he had some sensitive information, it is hard to see why.

CHAPTER X

The Third Story: The Trotskyite-Zinovievite Terrorist Center

The story before the public was now that Nikolayev had committed his crime as one of a group of Zinovievites, his success being charged to NKVD negligence; and that Zinoviev and Kamenev and the other former opposition leaders, while not directly responsible, had by their attitudes unwittingly encouraged the Leningrad group in its terrorism.

After the trials of the Moscow Center and of the Leningrad NKVD officers, 1935 passed comparatively peacefully, at least as far as the Kirov murder was concerned. There were indeed 'repressions' and tightening of Party discipline (both mild by later standards). But for a year and a half no new accusations about the murder were put out.

On 26 January 1935, Valerian Kuibyshev, who had sided with Kirov over the Ryutin and other cases, died. Three years later it was to be said that he was murdered on Yagoda's orders, but the evidence that it was anything but a heart attack is (as I write) slim—at any rate not proven.

Over the next months, a slow closing-in manifested itself, though on a scale which still left 1935 to be considered idyllic in comparison with later events. Maxim Gorky, who had stood for tolerance toward Old Bolsheviks, was attacked sharply in the press. Avel Yenukidze, Secretary of the Central Executive Committee and one of the oldest and most influential Bolsheviks, was suddenly expelled for "personal and political dissoluteness."

In the summer came the dissolution of the Society of Old Bolsheviks and the Society of Former Political Prisoners, both of which are reported as having collected signatures opposing the death penalty for the opposition.[1]

Meanwhile, legal changes presaged events to come. On 7 April a law was published which made children down to the age of twelve subject to all the same penalties as adults—a law that was later to be used to put pressure on arrested oppositionists in blackmailing them into confessions by threats against their young offspring.

On June 1935, a complementary law was published which, for the first time, held members of families responsible even if ignorant of their relations' crimes. True, this law applied only to deserters going abroad, but it was clearly capable of further development, which in fact happened when under the rubric 'Member of the Family of a Traitor to the Motherland' wives, children, and other relatives began receiving routine sentencing of five to eight years in camp, or even, on occasion, death.

The purge of the Party which had followed the Kirov murder continued with a secret circular letter on further 'verification' on 13 May. About a quarter of the membership were expelled on various grounds, though for the time being few were arrested. The measures taken in 1935 were in fact largely a matter of tightening the pressure, and implying the possibilities, rather than of taking immediate action. At the same time, administrative reorganization suitable to further repression took place. Yezhov became a member of the Secretariat. Vyshinsky became Prosecutor-General of the USSR.

In the summer a plot on Stalin's life was allegedly discovered. No charge was ever publicly laid, but it is believed that there was some truth in the story—involving a woman employee in the Kremlin library. Among the forty-odd persons arrested was Kamenev (whose brother was a doctor in the Kremlin), and of him alone we know officially that he was sentenced on 27 July 1935 to ten years imprisonment.[2] Yezhov and others are reported as arguing for the death penalty.[3]

Toward the end of the year the NKVD arrested a group of young Communists in the city of Gorky. It appears that they had spoken vaguely of assassinating Stalin. This would now have automatically meant an immediate death sentence. But the case was held over, on orders from Moscow. By February 1936 it was developed further. Olberg, an NKVD agent in the Gorky Pedagogical Institute, where the students worked, was turned into a Trotskyite. A former member of the NKVD Foreign Department, he had indeed served in Berlin as a secret informer on Trotskyite circles.[4] The case was now chosen as the core of a new plot, involving Trotskyites as well as Zinovievites. Several other lesser figures, including Zinoviev's former secretary, R. V. Pickel, were now arrested, and by May were giving suitable confessions.

A conference of some forty senior NKVD officers is reported as being instructed to investigate the newly discovered conspiracy. It was made clear that there was no question of finding the prisoners innocent, and that the duty of the interrogators was not to discover the facts but to fabricate, and impose, confessions. As the NKVD men involved were heads, or high officials, of the key State Security Departments, and had never come across the slightest evidence of the alleged plot, it was quite clear that the accused were innocent.[5] In fact, everyone concerned with the August 1936 trial knew this. Stalin and the NKVD interrogators knew it just as well as the victims. It was an elaborate farce in which a set of complex falsehoods were set in motion for political reasons.

Zinoviev, Kamenev, Evdokimov, and Bakayev were brought back from their isolators to face a new interrogation, with the veteran I. N. Smirnov serving as the senior Trotskyite.

When enough minor figures were confessing, pressure was brought to bear on Zinoviev and Kamenev. They were told that they were required to confess to having themselves actually planned the murder of Kirov. At first they refused. In May and June Zinoviev "made obdurate denials"; Bakayev made "persistent denials," as did others.[6]

Zinoviev and Kamenev were physically worn down—not by torture (though some of their juniors seem not to have been so lucky). But constant interrogation, inadequate food, overheated cells, and failure to treat Zinoviev's liver condition began to tell.[7]

One of the interrogators of Zinoviev and Kamenev was Lyushkov, who later defected to the Japanese. He tells us that he received instructions on the confessions required from Yezhov, who got them from Stalin.[8]

On one account Yezhov told Zinoviev that Soviet intelligence were certain that Germany and Japan would attack the USSR in the spring of 1937. In the circumstances it was necessary to destroy Trotskyism politically. Zinoviev must help by publicly "disarming" and implicating Trotsky too. Otherwise, Yezhov said, Zinoviev and the others would be shot after a closed trial, and all their former supporters would likewise suffer. Kamenev, in addition, was threatened with the death of his young son.[9] They made a condition that neither they nor their supporters would be executed, and Stalin personally assured them of this, adding that in unmasking Trotsky they would be doing such a service to the Party that they would earn only gratitude.

On this basis, they agreed to go to trial and by mid-July were giving satisfactory evidence to the interrogators. Evdokimov, who this time appears to have behaved with exceptional firmness, and to have been treated roughly, held out longer. But by 10 August he, too, had broken down.

The Indictment was published on 15 August, and on 19 August the trial opened—the first 'public' trial in the Kirov case actually to be held in public, with representatives of the Western press and diplomatic corps present.

There had previously been a few cases of this kind, never yet wholly successful. In 1928 Stalin had set up the Shakhty Trial of engineers: but there had been refusals to confess, withdrawals of evidence, embarrassing announcements of sudden deaths of the accused. In 1933 the 'Metro-Vic' Trial against British and Russian engineers had not been a real success, when the British accused, who had confessed while in the hands of the Secret Police, withdrew their confessions in court and denounced the whole proceedings.

But even these cases had deceived some observers, and some

foreigners. The new production in August 1936 was better prepared, and, on the whole, had a better reception.

The trial took place in the small 'October Hall' of the Trade Union House, formerly one of the ballrooms of the Nobles' Club. Ulrikh was once again chairman of the Military Collegium, with Matulevich and Nikitchenko (later to serve as the Soviet representative on the Nuremberg Tribunal) as the other members. Vyshinsky prosecuted.

This time Zinoviev, Kamenev, Evdokimov, and Bakayev together with I. N. Smirnov, Ter-Vaganyan, and Mrachkovsky to represent the 'Trotskyite' element, formed the 'Trotskyite–Zinovievite Terrorist Center'. Nine lesser defendants were there as links to Trotsky or organizers of more recent terrorist gangs.

The charges were of having plotted a terrorist campaign with Trotsky; of organizing terrorist groups to kill "Stalin, Voroshilov, Kaganovich, Kirov, Ordzhonikidze, Zhdanov, Kossior, Postyshev, and others"[10] and of having actually—through the Nikolayev group—succeeded in murdering Kirov. The Gestapo was also involved, though this was not greatly stressed.[11]

At far as the Kirov case went, the charge was that "one of these terrorist groups, operating on the direct instructions of Zinoviev and Trotsky and of the united Trotskyite-Zinovievite Center, and under the immediate direction of the accused Bakayev, carried out the foul murder of Comrade S. M. Kirov on December 1, 1934."[12]

Trotsky had allegedly sent terrorist instructions to Smirnov in 1931 even before the Zinovievites adopted that policy; and only in 1932 did the groups come to an understanding on the various plots that ensued. The Zinovievites had nevertheless handled the Kirov murder itself (though a single unnamed "Trotskyite terrorist" was alleged to have helped Bakayev).[13] The "bloc" is indeed represented as jointly having as a "main object . . . the assassination of the leaders of the CPSU, and in the first place the assassination of Stalin and Kirov."[14] But the accused fall into different categories quite apart from their membership or otherwise of the "Center," naturally dividing into Zinovievites and Trotskyites. The former, apart from Zinoviev, Kamenev, Evdokimov, and Bakayev, include Pickel, Reingold, and (partly) M. Lurye.

The Trotskyites, apart from Smirnov, Mrachkovsky, Ter-Vaganyan, and Dreitser consist of no fewer than five terrorists sent by Trotsky from abroad. In their case all the "instructions" allegedly received from Trotsky himself speak of removing "Stalin and Voroshilov"; "Stalin, Kaganovich, Voroshilov, and Ordzhonikidze"; "Zhdanov, Kaganovich, Ordzhonikidze, Kossior, and Postyshev" (or, in the case of individual terrorists, one or other of these, usually Stalin).[15] Why there was this comparative distancing of Trotsky from the Kirov murder (with the exception, as we shall note, of a single Trotskyite present at one of the plotters' meetings) is hard to say. It is true that Leningrad was an ex-Zinovievite fief; that Kirov had protected ex-Zinovievites rather than Trotskyites; that in the larger Stalin–Trotsky confrontation, Kirov might seem to loom small.

Not only was the Kirov murder still a predominantly Zinovievite crime but Zinoviev had confessed, according to Vyshinsky in his closing speech, that "he was pressing to hasten the murder. He was in a hurry, he clutched feverishly at people like Nikolayev and Kotolynov,. in order to hasten this murder. Not the least motive was to forestall the Trotskyite terrorists. The Trotskyites were pressing hard . . . Zinoviev declared that it was 'a matter of honor' . . . to carry out this criminal design sooner than the Trotskyites."[16]

We will not deal here with all the ramifications of the trial, with its variety of assassins seeking out victims among the whole leading cadre,[17] but only with its handling of the Kirov murder—which was, indeed, very much a central theme.

As against the mere moral and political responsibility of Zinoviev and the others presented in the January 1935 trial, this time it was a matter of their having actually masterminded the whole affair: (and their confessions at the earlier trial were now denounced as a hypocritical cover-up). So the world, or some of its representatives, saw Lenin's closest collaborators insisting on their guilt. The great orator Zinoviev made a complete and abject confession. Kamenev and most of the others followed suit.

As to the mechanism of the plot, Evdokimov, who confessed that he had "deceived the Court" in the 1933 trial,[18] said that a conference had been held in Kamenev's flat in the summer of 1934. He was present with Kamenev, Zinoviev, Sokolnikov, Ter-Vaganyan, Reingold, and Bakayev when "it was decided to expedite the assassination of S. M. Kirov"—Ter-Vaganyan being the one 'Trotskyite' involved at any point.[19] Or, as Evdokimov put it in another context, "In 1934 Zinoviev, acting in the name of the Trotskyite–Zinovievite organization, gave Bakayev direct instructions to organize the murder of Kirov."[20] He added that in 1934 Bakayev was sent by Zinoviev to contact Kotolynov and his group, with this murder in view.[21]

Bakayev's direct responsibility was to kill Stalin, and he was to organize the Kirov assassination through Karev.[22] Gertik had also contacted Kotolynov for this purpose.[23] Zinoviev, too, confirmed that Bakayev was in charge of both operations.[24] Bakayev's chief contact was allegedly Levin, now described as having been "the leader of the Leningrad terrorist underground organization."[25]

Levin called a meeting for him of the two of them, Mandelstam, Sositsky, Rumyantsev, Kotolynov, and Myasnikov. Through them he met Nikolayev, described by Levin as someone "Evdokimov had known for many years and whom he had given the best recommendation." Bakayev found Nikolayev a suitable assassin, "a man of determination." Nikolayev confirmed that he "with two other terrorists" was "keeping a watch on Kirov."[26]

As Vyshinsky put it in his final speech, "Bakayev heard the report of Leonid Nikolayev . . . and gave him and his accomplices a number of practical instructions concerning the organization of the assassination of Comrade S. M. Kirov."[27]

Kamenev had also been in touch, through Bakayev, with Tolmazov and Shatsky, of the original accomplices of Nikolayev.[28] He was also said in Vyshinsky's final speech to have gone to Leningrad in June 1934 (on the instructions of the Trotskyite–Zinovievite Center) to conduct "negotiations with the leader of one of the Leningrad terrorist groups, Yakovlev, whose case has been set aside for a separate trial, about the organization of this terrorist act against Comrade Kirov."[29]

Yakovlev was produced as a 'witness'. He worked in the Academy of Sciences, which was in Leningrad until December 1934, and with Karev formed a counterrevolutionary group. Kamenev commissioned him to "organize a terrorist group at the Academy of Sciences." He was "to prepare an attempt on the life of Kirov parallel with that of the Rumyantsev–Kotolynov group."[30] Another Leningrad academic, Friedland (elsewhere identified as a professor at the Leningrad Institute of Marxism), was among those under interrogation,[31] and his name is mentioned in passing, as a Trotskyite rather than Zinovievite terrorist, in Ter-Vaganyan's evidence,[32] although no connection is made either to the Kirov assassination or to Leningrad.

Apart from the main story of the direct guilt of Zinoviev and the others for the Kirov murder, the most significant new lead was an assertion that the Leningrad Zinovievites had been in the confidence of "a number of leading Party workers and officials of Soviet organizations in Leningrad," which had ensured them the possibility of preparing a terrorist act "without the least fear of being discovered."[33] (We shall pursue this theme, which was little noted at the time, in our next chapter.)

The case did not proceed entirely smoothly. Even the connections between the Moscow plotters and their Leningrad terrorist gang were a little muddled. At one point Karev was in charge of the plot against Stalin, at another of that against Kirov.[34] Sometimes Kotolynov and Rumyantsev were the leaders of the Leningrad group, sometimes Levin, and this apart from the mysterious Yakolev.

Even the confessions were not all quite satisfactory. The leading 'Trotskyite' accused, I. N. Smirnov, several times refused to corroborate the story, and denied that any 'Center' existed. There were even errors concerning Western fact. A conspiratorial meeting was described as taking place in the Hotel Bristol in Copenhagen, which had in fact been demolished in 1917.[35]

Not so much a contradiction but at least an oddity was that of the nineteen Zinovievites accused at the previous trial, only four were produced—even though several others were named. Kuklin was described as actually a member of the new 'Center'.[36] Karev, whose evidence was freely quoted, was named as the original direct organizer of the Kirov murder—but his case was "set aside for separate trial," together with that of Faivilovich,[37] identified as also maintaining organizational contact with the Leningrad group.[38] Gertik's case, too, was set aside, though he also had contacted Kotolynov in connection with the preparations for Kirov's murder.[39] Gaven, who had brought Trotsky's instructions, likewise failed to appear. He was shot on 4 October,[40] reportedly carried to execution on a stretcher because of his tuberculosis.[41] (The only other known death date of those involved in these cases without public announcement of their execution is, as I write, that of P. A. Zalutsky on 19 January 1937).[42]

Some obvious blemishes in the prosecution case had been, it is reported, represented to Stalin by Agranov—in particular the impossibility that Smirnov, in jail, could have conspired after January 1933. Agranov suggested that the West would not be deceived. Stalin is said to have answered contemptuously "They'll swallow it."[43]

Stalin's assessment was, up to a point, sound. The trial caused a worldwide sensation. Few Westerners could make head or tail of the phenomenon of the confessions. But the charge of assassinating Kirov, and planning to assassinate Stalin, was not all that implausible. Kirov was, or had been, a political foe. He and the whole Stalin group had removed Zinoviev and Kamenev from power. The Zinovievites had no other obvious method of struggle left to them. The Marxist-Leninist view that individual assassination was to be avoided might no longer apply.

But if an assassination plot was plausible enough, the abject self-abasement by the 'defendants' and their acceptance not only of their guilt but also of the wrongness of their actions did not seem convincing. Yet they showed no signs of having been tortured. And, as in later trials, while some Westerners believed the whole story, others felt that the charges, though exaggerated, were not wholly false.

Moreover, many in the Western left were already emotionally involved in support for the Soviet Union as a supposed bastion against fascism—a feeling which became stronger with the outbreak of the Spanish Civil War on 18 July. Even if dubious about the trial, they did not feel the issue to be as urgent, and preferred not to hear it raised. Thus, in one way or another, and even apart from the disciplined credulity of the not inconsiderable body of Western Communists proper, Stalin's calculations proved fairly well founded.

As we have noted, Zinoviev and the others are reported as having been promised their lives by Stalin personally if they went through the public trial.[44] However, once this was over, they had no sanction to make him carry out his side of the bargain.

As a special encouragement to the accused, the right to appeal had been allowed them—which is to say that the procedural decree of 1 December 1934 was not applied. On 25 August it was announced they had indeed appealed, that the appeals had been rejected, and that all the accused had been shot.

But they were not the last to be officially blamed for the assassination of Kirov. Another and even stranger story was to come.

CHAPTER XI

The Fate of the Kirovites

Eighteen months were to pass before the next version of the murder plot was to be put to the world by Stalin's courts. Meanwhile, and especially by the spring of 1937, the mass terror struck the populace and the Party alike.

Alleged direct participants in the Kirov murder could be found outside Leningrad. For example, Karl Brandt, first secretary of a district committee in Kharkov, was arrested in 1937 and shot on 23 August 1938 by order of an NKVD Special Board for "literally . . . participating in the terrorist group which prepared and carried out the murder of Kirov." His wife got twenty years as "wife of an enemy of the people."[1]

People totally unconnected with Kirov, or Leningrad, might also be accused of being accomplices in the murder simply on the basis of sharing the views of the terrorists. And, as in the case of Evgenia Ginzburg, this could happen to those who had never had the slightest inclination to Zinovievite, Trotskyite, or other oppositionist views. The new victims were in one way or another implicated in the Trotskyite–Zinovievite–Rightist bourgeois-nationalist conspiracies (entered into in collaboration with the Nazi, the Polish, the Japanese, the British, and other espionage services), whose murder of Kirov had been their most important and characteristic crime. In the end, millions must have been accomplices, at least to this extent, in the murder.

It is not the purpose of this book to consider the terror which struck the Party and the population, the Army and the intellectuals, and imposed the Stalin regime in its fullest form, though we can stress once again that the Kirov murder can be seen as the key event which made such a denouement possible. Here we will consider mainly the fate of Kirov's Leningrad followers, which has an obvious bearing on what we have already recorded.

At the August 1936 trial of the 'Trotskyite–Zinovievite Terrorist Center', as we noted and should now register more fully, it was stated in passing that "such active Zinovievites as Rumyantsev, Levin, Myasnikov, Mandelstam, and others enjoyed the confidence of a number of leading Party workers and officials of Soviet organizations in Leningrad. This ensured them every possibility of pursuing their preparations for a terrorist act against Kirov without the least fear of being discovered." This aside, though little remarked, was to be of sinister significance to the Kirovite machine in Leningrad. The reference to officials of "Soviet organizations" might possibly indicate the NKVD; but the "leading Party workers" could only mean some, at least, of the most prominent of Kirov's men, still in position after the assassination.

At the same time, an attack appeared on the leaders of a key Leningrad district—the Vyborg 'raion'—where "Trotskyites and Zinovievites expelled from the party were able, thanks to the rotten district committee liberals, to be reinstated in the Party. They were able to deceive the Party because in the district organizations there are still blind people, there are still stupid people, who can be led by the nose: that is, in fact, direct accomplices of these swine."[2] This is in fact typical of the assaults on local and subordinate organizations and individuals which were to mark a Stalinist technique of compromising and isolating their superiors.

Chudov, presumably held responsible as Second Secretary, that is in charge of cadres, was removed in July 1936, and replaced by Zhdanov's adherent and brother-in-law, the notorious A. A. Shcherbakov.[3] Chudov was apparently transferred to Moscow, to a minor post in the Trade Union apparat.[4] The other Leningrader who seems to have been demoted at this point is Struppe, Chairman of the Provincial Executive Committee until 1936,[5] who is reported now being made Head of the Pig-Rearing Directorate in the People's Commissariat of State Farms.[6] For the moment, other top Kirovites kept their posts.

Kodatsky strove to fit in with the new Stalinist spirit. At this time a Leningrad NKVD man called Drovyanikov, at a meeting of the local NKVD party aktiv, complained that conspiracies were being fabricated; Kodatsky attacked him as an enemy who showed that "enemies of the people both infiltrated the NKVD and needed to be ruthlessly eradicated."[7] Kodatsky was a member of the Drafting Commission for the New Constitution, named on the second anniversary of Kirov's death.[8]

But in May 1937, Zhdanov told the Leningrad aktiv that "two enemies—Chudov and Kodatsky—have been exposed in our ranks, in the Leningrad organization. They have been arrested in Moscow." One of those present comments, "it was as if our tongues were frozen." But, she says, she found the courage to intervene after the session, going up to Zhdanov and complaining: "Comrade Zhdanov, I don't know Chudov. He hasn't been in our Leningrad organization long. But I vouch for Kodatsky. He has been a Party member since 1913. I have known him for many years. He is an honest member of the Party. He fought all the oppositionists. This is incredible!" Zhdanov looked at her "with his cruel eyes" and said "Lazurkina, stop this talk, otherwise it will end badly for you."[9]

Chudov and Kodatsky had, of course, been Kirov's chief subordinates and closest collaborators, and more than anyone else represented the Kirov tradition in Leningrad. Chudov, a printing worker, had joined the Party in 1913. With Stalin, Molotov, Voroshilov, and Zhdanov he had been one of the honorary bearers at Kirov's lying-in-state in Leningrad.[10] Kodatsky, as we have seen, had worked with Kirov in Astrakhan in 1919, and served him loyally until his death.[11]

A 'case' was already being prepared against N. P. Komarov, Zinoviev's successor as Chairman of the Leningrad Soviet and Executive Committee in Kirov's first years in the city, from 1926 to 1929. Though then transferred and demoted to Head of the Rural Cooperatives, as inadequately hard on the Rightists in the city, he had remained a candidate member of the Central Committee.

One of those implicated in Komarov's case was an old Party member called Rozenblum. Zakovsky was in charge of this investigation, which appears to have linked the Kirov apparatus with the alleged 'Rightist' consiprators. After "terrible torture" Rozenblum was brought before him. Zakovsky told him that he was to be a witness in a new trial, of "sabotage, espionage, and diversion in a terroristic center in Leningrad," in which the accused would include Chudov, Ugarov, Smorodin, Pozern, and Chudov's wife Lyudmila Shaposhnikova,[12] deputy chairman and secretary of the Leningrad trade unions,[13] with "two or three others."

"In order to illustrate it to me," stated Rozenblum, "Zakovsky gave me several possible variants of the organization of this center and of its branches." Zakovsky went on to explain to Rozenblum:

> The case of . . . the Leningrad center has to be built solidly and for this reason witnesses are needed. . . . You yourself will not need to invent anything. The NKVD will prepare for you a ready outline for every branch of the center; you will have to study it carefully and to remember well all questions and answers which the court might ask. This case will be ready in four or five months or perhaps a half year. During this time you will be preparing yourself so that you will not compromise the investigation and yourself. Your future will depend on how the trial goes and on its results. If you begin to lie and to testify falsely, blame yourself. If you manage to endure it, you will save your head and we will feed and clothe you at the government's cost until your death.[14]

What the 'terrorist center' would have been accused of is not specified. But almost all such alleged conspiracies throughout the country were, in one way or another, linked with the murder of Kirov. So, such a connection is virtually certain, and in the case of Chudov and the others one may safely conclude a more direct involvement, and their identification with the 'leading Party workers and officials of Soviet organizations in Leningrad,' whose confidence Levin, Rumyantsev, and the others had enjoyed. This would mean that Kirov's closest chosen associates were now amongst those supposedly among the sponsors of his assassination. Their real crime, it might seem, was the opposite one of being Kirovite.

The NKVD mounted public trials, such as Zakovsky planned, in Georgia and elsewhere. The public access was often largely imaginary, though, particularly in local small-town cases, such performances are sometimes reported as made in front of genuine audiences—not always with complete success. But only in the three 'Moscow Trials' were foreigners, diplomats, and journalists admitted. It may have been intended to have a Leningrad trial with some public attendance, perhaps even with international observers, or at least public announcement.

But the case, in which the list of accused included men who were still at liberty and in responsible positions, was abandoned, at least in this form.

Chudov and Kodatsky were shot on 30 October 1937, a day which also saw the execution of at least fifteen other senior officials, including thirteen other former members of the Central Committee; (Komarov, however, was not shot until 27 November, also with a number of other high officials).[15]

We do not at present have Struppe's precise death date. But he is given as dying during 1937,[16] so perhaps perished with Chudov and Kodatsky. Lyudmila Shaposhnikova was only sentenced to eight years as a "member of the family of a traitor to the motherland," and sent to prison in Tomsk, though reportedly brought back and shot in 1938.[17] There is no doubt that Stalin initiated or approved these arrests, and that the death warrants were among the 40,000-odd he signed personally in 1937–1938.

The fate of Ugarov, Pozern, and Smorodin, already compromised in Zakovsky's new Leningrad terrorist center, well indicates the extraordinary obliqueness of Stalin's approach. They were at first merely removed from the Leningrad apparatus. By late 1937 Pozern had become the Province's Prosecutor, a severe demotion.[18] He had been editing a biography of Kirov, which reached its third volume in 1937 (going up to the year 1926); thereafter no further volumes appeared.[19] He was still at liberty in February 1938, but was arrested later in the year.[20] Pozern's condition after interrogation—he was an older man than his co-accused and a Party member since 1903—is described by a survivor, M. R. Maek.

Maek was a junior official who had worked in the Leningrad Provincial Committee apparatus. When arrested, he was shown a deposition from Pozern that he had recruited Maek into his counterrevolutionary organization. Maek demanded a confrontation. Many years later, after his release and rehabilitation, Maek described how "an utterly emaciated old man entered the investigation office, whom he hardly recognised as Pozern. Maek asked him, 'How, Boris Pavlovich, how could you write such ridiculous stuff, that you recruited me to an anti-Soviet organisation?' But Pozern, looking down, began suddenly to say: 'It doesn't matter, it doesn't matter, my friend; I recruited you, I recruited you.' Everything was immediately clear to Maek."[21]

Smorodin was sent as First Secretary to Stalingrad in August 1937, a promotion. A. I. Ugarov became Leningrad's Second Secretary by 1937 (on Shcherbakov's promotion elsewhere). He was actually transferred from Leningrad to Moscow in 1938 to take the place of Khrushchev, who had been moved to the Ukraine. As First Secretary of the Moscow Party organization, Ugarov appeared on the highest platforms until the autumn of 1938.

Pozern, Ugarov, and Smorodin were all under arrest by the end of that year. And all were shot on the same day, 25 February 1939, part of a large massacre of leading figures over 22–26 February.[22] Most of the others perished on the other days of this operation, and it is reasonably clear that processing Pozern, Smorodin, and Ugarov together means a 'Leningrad Case', finally winding up the whole Kirov regime in the city. By one of the many ironies of the Stalin period, Zakovsky seems to have been shot among the same week's victims.[23] So was Kosarev.

These are names whose fates we can follow. Of others, we know less. Of the forty names which appear on a Kirov obituary statement by Leningraders in *Pravda* of 2 December 1934, there are a number we cannot trace further. But those we can trace are mostly identifiable as having been shot—in particular the eleven top names, starting with Chudov. That is to say, a clean sweep was made of the leading Kirov apparat.

In 1934 there were, apart from Kirov, seven Leningrad members or candidate members of the Central Committee. All perished—the five we have named in the two shootings of October 1937 and February 1939, plus Struppe and P. A. Alekseyev, Head of the Leningrad Trade Unions, together with the Leningrad member of the lesser Central Revision Commission I. I. Alekseyev, Party Secretary at the legendary Putilov (later Kirov) works, the bastion of the Revolution.[24]

Others arrested as "enemies of the people" included four more who had served under Kirov as secretaries of the provincial committee—P. A. Irklis (Secretary in charge of supply, and so presumably the man Stalin attacked in 1934: see p. 32), A. V. Osipov, P. L. Nizovtsev, and A. A. Nikulov. Other victims included Struppe's predecessor as Chairman of the Provincial Executive Committee, F. F. Tsarkov; the Chairmen of the Provincial and of the City Collegia of Party Control, V. A. Shestakov and A. I. Kiselev; and the Secretary of the Leningrad Young Communist League, I. S. Vayshlya.[25] Indeed almost the whole of the Leningrad Party's active cadres, even at a lower level, were struck down. As one of them, a survivor of seventeen years in camp, said later "I had an executive post in the Leningrad Province Party Committee and, of course, was also arrested."[26] So were, for example, A. I. Abramov, who had been Head of the Leningrad Party's organization department,[27] leading apparatchiks S. M. Sobolev, M. V. Bogdanov, "and others,"[28] plus Levitt, Head of the Party department at *Leningradskaya Pravda*.[29]

The heads of the Leningrad districts were also shot—Brigadnyy and Vasilev, Chairmen of the Novgorod and Akulov District Executive Committees, along with others.[30] We are told that "hundreds of active party and Soviet workers" went.[31] Even of the sixty-five members of the new City Committee elected in May 1937, only two remained in June 1938.

The leading industrialists, Kirov's special protégés, also went to the slaughter. In particular his favorite M. K. Ots, Head of the

Putilov Works; I. N. Penkin, Head of the Metallik Works; I. F. Antyukhin, Head of Lenenergo;[32] Kondrikiv, Head of Appetot Trust.[33]

Under Stalin, Zhdanov was in fact doing as radical a job on the Kirovites as Kirov had done on the Zinovievites when it came to removing the previous cadres of leadership: though this time the removal involved physical annihilation. (In 1949–1950, the Zhdanovites in their turn were to go to the execution cellars in a later 'Leningrad Case'.)

The Leningrad First Secretary in Khrushchev's time described the events:

> The Leningrad Party organization suffered particularly large losses of Party, Soviet, economic, and other personnel as a result of the unjustified repressions that befell Leningrad after the murder of Sergei Mironovich Kirov. For a period of four years there was an uninterrupted wave of repressions in Leningrad against honest and completely innocent people. Promotion to a responsible post often amounted to a step toward the brink of a precipice. Many people were annihilated without a trial and investigation on the basis of false, hastily fabricated charges. Not only officials themselves but also their families were subjected to repressions, even absolutely innocent children, whose lives were thus broken from the very beginning.[34]

Kirov is described as always very careful about his selection of personnel; and, we can have no doubt, these Leningraders were his own men to the core.[35] That all his aides and assistants thus perished presumably has some bearing on the crime, if only as an indication of Stalin's attitude to the Kirov tradition.

One of the handful of junior Leningraders to remain and prosper was A. A. Kuznetsov, who was to become Zhdanov's successor as Leningrad First Secretary, and to be shot in the later 'Leningrad Case' of 1949–1950. A recent Soviet article gives as evidence of the naïveté and boldness of his character that he "openly" visited Kirov's widow Maria (who had gone mad after her husband's death); and that he kept "photographs of Sergei Mironovich (although Stalin's attitude to him was no big secret for many people even at that time)."[36]

CHAPTER XII

The Fourth Story:
The Rightists and the NKVD

While the Leningraders and the vast majority of the other victims of the terror disappeared without public notice, two more open trials followed that of Zinoviev and his accomplices. The second of these great trials, that of 'the Anti-Soviet Trotskyite Center' took place in January 1937. Little was said about the Kirov case.

Pyatakov, Radek, and fifteen others were accused of having been a 'Reserve Center' kept secret in case the Zinoviev plotters were discovered. The group shot in August 1936 were now accused of having deceived the court by concealing this second network.

This time, the conspiracy went further than just assassination. A vast amount of industrial sabotage, in mines, railways, chemical works, and elsewhere, was alleged against the accused, together with treason and espionage.

When it came to the Kirov case, Karl Radek testified that in 1932, though no names were mentioned, he had gathered that terrorism was to be directed against "Stalin and his immediate colleagues, against Kirov, Molotov, Voroshilov, and Kaganovich."[1] He added that he had named a Trotskyite to assist the

Zinovievite plotters against Kirov—Prigozhin,[2] the Leningrad historian (former husband of the daughter of the head of the British Labour Party, George Lansbury), with "a group of three or four others."[3] Zeidel, another historian, was also mentioned.[4] But as these two and their group were said never to have taken action, this added little of substance.[5]

As has been pointed out, a number of Radek's remarks seem to have been subtle disclaimers. And as to the efficacy of terrorism, he said "when we first gathered together after the murder of Kirov, there arose the question that it was senseless to kill individuals."[6] The results had been poor, and included "arrests of a large number of Zinovievites and Trotskyites."[7] And in his final speech he declared that the assassination seemed to be "without any political advantage to ourselves."[8]

In his closing speech for the prosecution, Vyshinsky virulently attacked Pyatakov and the others as implicated in the Kirov murder. But apart from the addition of these new conspirators, the official story remained unchanged.

In February 1937, Bukharin and Rykov, leaders of the 'Rightists', were arrested.

Yagoda was arrested in April 1937. With him, or shortly afterwards, went his subordinates, including (of those featuring in this story) Agranov, Volovich, and Mironov (though not as yet Medved, Zaporozhets, and the Leningraders, still working in Kolyma). Except for Yagoda, and his secretary Bulanov, none was to appear in public again.

No major public trial was to take place until March 1938 when these two, and the Rightists and a large selection of others, were to appear before the Military Collegium. Meanwhile, apart from the publicly announced (though not public) trial of the leading officers of the Red Army in June 1937, the year passed without any demonstrative blow against the elements being liquidated by the terror: for example, as we have said, from the point of view of the public Chudov and Kodatsky simply disappeared.

Or rather, there was a trial of important figures announced, but not held in public, in December 1937. There are a number of interesting features about this 'trial'. Though it was announced that Avel Yenukidze and the others concerned had been tried on 16 December 1937, and had confessed their guilt, those we can trace are all given in modern Soviet reference books as having died earlier (in Yenukidze's case on 30 October), which would account for the December trial not being held in public.

The public trial of Bukharin, Yagoda, and others opened on 2 March 1938. A broad array of crimes was charged against them. From the point of view of the Kirov case the first point is that Bukharin and the Rightists were now shown to have formed part of the Trotskyite-Zinovievite conspiracy from the start. In the Kirov assassination, their role had been, through Yagoda (now exposed as a Rightist), to have used the NKVD to facilitate Nikolayev's access to Kirov.

Although Bukharin and the others admitted their membership in the 'bloc', Bukharin and Rykov both refused to confess complicity in the Kirov murder. Bukharin in his last plea said, "I categorically deny my complicity in the assassination of Kirov"; and Rykov also denied it.[9] However, they were found guilty on this charge, and this verdict entered the Stalinist canon.

From our point of view, however, the main interest of the trial was that it was now that the NKVD was first publicly blamed not for mere negligence but for active complicity in the crime. The mechanism was that Yagoda had indeed procured the murder. But what was Yagoda's motive? Or failing that, who forced him to the murder? Who among the NKVD, or who else in the political leadership capable of sponsoring an NKVD involvement, had the slightest interest in killing Kirov? Even the Stalinist version has some difficulty with this, making the almost ostentatiously harmless and uninvolved Yenukidze the villain who had given Yagoda his instructions on behalf of the Center.

Yenukidze (who had been Chairman of Kirov's funeral commission) was never a 'Rightist', but he seems to have shared Kirov's distaste for intraparty repression. We can be fairly sure that he had not himself confessed to the charges made in the Bukharin Trial, even though these often involved him deeply. For, in spite of one reference to his having 'confirmed' that he had ordered Yagoda to facilitate the Kirov murder, no quotation whatever from his supposed confession is given at any point. It is true that he and Zaporozhets are said to have confirmed Yagoda's evidence "during the investigation," but nothing is quoted from either.[10]

In the announcement of Yenukidze's own 'trial' in court in December 1937, following his execution in October, the organizers had had a free hand as to what was alleged. But the assassination of Kirov had not been raised, nor was it in a much longer denunciation of the crimes of Yenukidze in a speech by Frinovsky, the Deputy People's Commissar of the NKVD, on 20 December. There Yenukidze is cited merely as a "member of the Trotskyite and Bukharinite espionage and terrorist organization," with no reference to the Kirov case.[11] This presumably means that the story to be presented in the great trial in three months time had not yet been decided on.

Report in the Kolyma area was that Medved and most of the Leningraders were arrested around December 1937, and taken back to Moscow and shot; Zaporozhets remained briefly after the others had gone.[12] If this account is true, it may mean that the decision to charge Zaporozhets was also taken fairly late in the 'investigative' proceedings.

It is also the case that in the interrogations of Yagoda referred to in the court proceedings, the Kirov evidence comes late (Vol. II, p. 209 of the investigation) after other alleged acts of terror (pp. 141–42, 193, 200).[13]

There is thus reason to believe that Stalin only decided to tell the story of Yagoda's and Zaporozhets's connection with the murder around the beginning of 1938. (Just as the decision to accuse Bukharin of having planned the murder of Lenin in 1918 only seems to have been added to the Indictment in February 1938.)[14] An NKVD source suggests that Stalin only learned quite late both of the suspicions aroused by the admitted NKVD 'negligence' and of the knowledge circulating in limited circles of Zaporozhets's involvement—no one having dared to tell him.[15] If so, it could account for the introduction of the Kirov theme into the new trial.

In court, Yagoda testified that Yenukidze had told him that "the center of the 'bloc of Rights and Trotskyites' had adopted a decision to organize the assassination of Kirov":

I tried to object, I marshalled a series of arguments about this terrorist act being inexpedient and unnecessary. I even argued that I, as a person responsible for guarding members of the government, would be the first to be held responsible in case a terrorist act was committed against a member of the government. Needless to say, my objections were not taken into consideration and had no effect. Yenukidze insisted that I was not to place any obstacles in the way; the terrorist act, he said, would be carried out by the Trotskyite–Zinovievite group.[16]

Similar phrasing about Yenudikze giving orders to Yagoda and overruling his objections are repeated in Vyshinsky's speech for the prosecution.[17] But of course Yenukidze's status in 'insisting' that Yagoda do anything at all was nil: he was far less powerful than Yagoda was. . . .

Yagoda was thus "compelled to instruct Zaporozhets, who occupied the post of Assistant Chief of the Regional Administration of the People's Commissariat of Internal Affairs not to place any obstacles in the way of the terrorist act against Kirov."[18]

After Yagoda had given instructions to Zaporozhets, the latter came to Moscow[19] to report to him that "the organization of the People's Commissariat of Internal Affairs had detained Nikolayev, in whose possession a revolver and a chart of the route Kirov usually took had been found. Nikolayev was released."[20] Or, as Vyshinsky put it in his closing speech, "Some two months before the assassination, Leonid Nikolayev was detained and brought to the Regional Administration. He was found to be in possession of a revolver and cartridges and a chart of the route that Kirov used to take. This made it perfectly clear that this scoundrel was preparing to commit a monstrous crime. But obeying the direct orders of Yagoda, Zaporozhets released this scoundrel, and two months later Nikolayev assassinated Kirov, committing this dastardly act with the direct participation of the contemptible traitor Yagoda, whose duty it was at that time to protect the persons of members of the government."[21]

Bulanov gave evidence that Yagoda told him early in 1936 that "he had known that an attempt on S. M. Kirov was being prepared, that he had had a reliable man in Leningrad who was initiated into everything, Zaporozhets, Assistant Chief of the Leningrad Regional Administration of the People's Commissariat of Internal Affairs, and that he so arranged matters as to facilitate the assassination of Kirov by Nikolayev. To put it plainly, it was done with the direct connivance, and consequently with the assistance, of Zaporozhets. I recall that Yagoda said in passing, incidentally abusing Zaporozhets for his lack of efficiency, that there was an occasion when the whole affair was nearly exposed, when several days before the assassination of Kirov the guard detained Nikolayev by mistake, and a notebook and revolver were found in his portfolio, but that Zaporozhets released him in time."[22]

Those in court witnessed a curious exchange between Vyshinsky and Yagoda:

Vyshinsky: After this, did you personally take any measures to effect the assassination of Sergei Mironovich Kirov?

Yagoda: I personally?

Vyshinsky: Yes, as a member of the bloc.

Yagoda: I gave instructions . . .

Vyshinsky: To whom?

Yagoda: To Zaporozhets in Leningrad. That is not quite how it was.

Vyshinsky: We shall speak about that later. What I want now is to elucidate the part played by Rykov and Bukharin in this villainous act.

Yagoda: I gave instructions to Zaporozhets. When Nikolayev was detained . . .

Vyshinksy: The first time?

Yagoda: Yes. Zaporozhets came to Moscow and reported to me that a man had been detained . . .

Vyshinsky: In whose briefcase . . .

Yagoda: There was a revolver and a diary. And he released him.

Vyshinsky: And you approved of this?

Yagoda: I just took note of the fact.

Vyshinsky: And then you gave instructions not to place obstacles in the way of the murder of Sergei Mironovich Kirov?

Yagoda: Yes, I did . . . It was not like that.

Vyshinsky: In a somewhat different form?

  Yagoda: It was not like that, but it is not important.

Vyshinsky: Did you give instructions?

  Yagoda: I have confirmed that.

Vyshinsky: You have. Be seated.[23]

As far as we can see, Yagoda seems to be hinting that something was wrong, or missing, in the story now before the court: but not that, as far as it went, it was untrue.

Even the earlier mild treatment of Zaporozhets, Medved, and the others was now, with apparent plausibility, attributed to Yagoda. Bulanov testified:

> I then understood the exceptional and unusual solicitude which Yagoda had displayed when Medved, Zaporozhets and the other officials were arrested and brought to trial. I recalled that he had entrusted the care of the families of Zaporozhets and Medved to me personally. I recalled that he had had them sent for detention to the camp in an unusual way, not in the car for prisoners, but in a special through car. Before sending them, he had Zaporozhets and Medved brought to see him.[24]

The murder of Borisov was also explained. Borisov also "had a share in the assassination of Kirov," and when he was to be brought as a witness Zaporozhets, "fearing that Borisov would betray" those behind the assassination, "arranged that an accident occurred to the automobile which took Borisov to the Smolny. Borisov was killed in the accident."[25]

Thus again, an incident too widely known for comfort was reinterpreted.

As to the number involved on the NKVD side, Zaporozhets, as we have said, is named as being one of those confessing during the investigation, though in the Indictment he is among those named as "the subject of separate proceedings."[26] It was also strongly suggested that Molchanov, Head of the NKVD Secret Political Department at the Center, was involved in the plot.[27]

Then, a reference was made to Yagoda giving "special instructions to his accomplices [note the plural] working in the Leningrad

Administration of the People's Commissariat of Internal Affairs not to hinder the perpetration of the crime."[28]

In sum, the key roles of Yagoda and Zaporozhets were now publicly established, though not in detail. And various facts from the December 1934 events were now publicly ventilated but, as it were, neutralized.

One problem for the independent observer was that almost all the rest of the confessions at the trial were obviously untrue, and this led to the suspicion that the Yagoda–Zaporozhets story was merely a further falsification designed to implicate Yagoda, and through him the Rightists. Thus, those who believed the trial thought that all the truth had been told, and those who did not believe it thought that no truth had been told. In neither case did this thinking tend to implicate Stalin. Still, we may note that not only did Bukharin and Rykov deny responsibility. But Yagoda, too, though his testimony in dock had been that he had transmitted Yenukidze's instructions to Zaporozhets, also said in his closing speech that "it is not only untrue to say that I was an organizer but it is untrue to say that I was an accomplice in the murder of Kirov. I committed an extremely grave violation of duty—that is right but I was not an accomplice."[29] He added that nothing in the court proceedings proved the contrary. This is so inconsistent with all the evidence that it might possibly be seen as an attempt to make the disavowals of the others sound implausible.

The Stalinist story, developed through four versions, had now reached its final form. In effect, what was henceforth to remain the official line was as follows:

1. Nikolayev had been a member of a group of Leningrad Zinovievites, who had actually organized the assassination.

2. They had done so on the orders of Zinoviev and his Moscow Center, carrying out a joint decision of the Trotskyite–Zinovievite Center, following instructions from Trotsky (though Trotsky's direct involvement, through the Latvian Consul, was dropped between 1934 and 1936).

3. The Rightists were also involved. Their role was to ensure through Yagoda, a member of the Rightist conspiracy, that the assassin had access to Kirov. Yagoda had received his instruc-

tions from Yenukidze, and passed them on to Zaporozhets who, with unspecified assistance, carried them out.

So, by this time all of Lenin's first leadership group, except for Stalin, were implicated in the murder: Trotsky (to be killed in 1940); Zinoviev and Kamenev; Bukharin, Rykov, and Tomsky. Sidney and Beatrice Webb's earlier comment, that Nikolayev had been "discovered to have secret connections with conspiratorial circles of ever widening range" was strikingly borne out.[30]

As Vyshinsky said in his closing speech, "this assassination was fully revealed and unmasked in the preceding trial, but it has only now been established that the activities of the Trotskyite–Zinovievite Center which murdered Sergei Mironovich Kirov were not of an independent character. It has now been established that Kirov was assassinated by decisions of this very Right–Trotskyite center, of this bloc, which may be called the center of all centers."[31]

CHAPTER XIII

Truths Emerge

For eighteen years no further story, and no further information, came from official sources. Over this period the increasing trickle of evidence, finally amounting to a reasonably full account, was unofficial. That is to say, it came from individuals who had access in one way or another to part of the facts concealed and distorted in the public literature.

Of course, there was considerable skepticism about the official story, at least in so far as it implicated the oppositionists. Yet the idea that Nikolayev was an individual assassin, with oppositionist motives, was plausible enough. And to implicate Stalin seemed in general to be as improbable as, or more improbable than, to attribute guilt to Zinoviev or Bukharin.

There were a few exceptions. As early as February 1935 Trotsky was writing that "The Zinoviev Case is a great smokescreen for the Stalin–Yagoda Case." It was clear, he said, that the Leningrad NKVD could not have given the assassin his opportunity without Yagoda's orders, and "without the direct agreement of Stalin—or more truly without his initiative—neither Yagoda nor Medved could ever have decided on such a risky undertaking."[1] By October 1936, he was putting it that "Stalin consequently bears not only the political, but also the direct responsibility for the murder of Kirov."[2]

Trotsky, however, took a special view of what Stalin had intended: that is, to prevent the assassination at the last moment and then proceed with the case against the oppositionists. This "playing with Kirov's head" went wrong owing to Nikolayev's "premature shot." This analysis seems to have been based not on any evidence but on the idea that Stalin, as a Marxist, would not undertake individual terror; or even that he would not wish his close colleagues killed. Both suppositions were, of course, to be proven incorrect over the next few years; and the use of 'individual terror' was to include the murder of Trotsky himself. Still, Trotsky had already proposed a mechanism for the case which implicated Stalin rather than the oppositionists.

Totsky's view was, in any case, a matter of deduction from the official record. The first unofficial evidence of some of the background, though not on the murder itself, came with the publication in 1936–1937 of the famous "Letter of an Old Bolshevik."

And here we must consider the whole question of evidence, both first-hand and second-hand (or third-hand). It is, of course, a truism of the criminal courts that even first-hand evidence is not always true. It may be totally false, in order to cover up the witness's own responsibility. It may be partly false, covering up some lesser fault of the witness, or merely presenting him in a more favorable light than is warranted (and this last may be a more or less unconscious distortion). It may be misleading because of uncontrolled imagination; or because of mere incapacity to observe correctly, or to remember accurately; and generally speaking the longer the period since the event, the greater the possible distortion.

Second-hand evidence is often all that is available in much historical research. It suffers, or may suffer, from all these varieties of falsehood or distortion. And, in addition, the second-hand testifier may have misunderstood his original informant. Except for the case of conscious falsification, none of these imperfections necessarily renders a given testimony valueless.

As Jane Austen wrote, "Seldom, very seldom, does complete truth belong to any human disclosure; seldom can it happen that something is not a little disguised or a little mistaken." It is the everyday duty of courts to extract the truth from evidence subject to a wide variety of imperfections. Historians have a similar duty. It might seem unnecessary to labor this point. But there has been a tendency—not so much among historians as among extraneous academics venturing into historical work for which they are unsuited—simply to label certain sources as 'unreliable' and then to dismiss them entirely. The true tests for such sources are found in the answers to two questions. First, is the provenance of a source traceable? Second, does a source confirm or fit in with—not necessarily in every detail—other evidence independent of its own?

"Letter of an Old Bolshevik" was in fact written by the Menshevik Boris Nicolaevsky. (The title was a late suggestion by the editor of *Sotsialisticheski Vestnik,* where it appeared in 1936–1937.) It was, in fact, based (as far as its information up to the summer of 1936 is concerned) on conversations Nicolaevsky had with Bukharin in May of that year. Nicolaevsky, who had been Head of the Marx–Engels Institute in Moscow in the early years of the Revolution, had in his charge highly important Marxist archives which he had brought to France from Germany in 1933. Bukharin had been sent with a view to examining and possibly purchasing this material. Nicolaevsky was a brother-in-law of Bukharin's closest associate, the former Soviet Premier, Aleksei Rykov.

There is nothing odd about political conversations between Bukharin and Nicolaevsky (though Bukharin would naturally not discuss state secrets). Pyatakov had had such a conversation with Valentinov-Volsky, whom he had met by chance in a Berlin street; and Bukharin was with Nicolaevsky on several occasions, for a fairly long time. Medvedev, indeed, argues that Bukharin would not have spoken with comparative freedom to Nicolaevsky.[3] But this is pure negative assumption. There is no reason whatever to think Nicolaevsky was romancing. (And Bukharin spoke in similar terms to another Menshevik, Lydia Dan.)

As far as we are concerned, the main value of the "Letter" lies in its definite assertions, first that Kirov opposed Stalin on the question of shooting Ryutin (a point much later confirmed in Soviet official literature), and that he had defended the ex-Zinovievite Komsomols in Leningrad and sponsored their historical work.

There is no information on the murder proper, though the "Letter" does give the first published information of the nugatory way in which the Leningrad NKVD officers were serving their sentences.

The first testimony connected with the murder came from Commissar of State Security Third Class G. S. Lyushkov, who defected to the Japanese in June 1938, when he was Head of the Far Eastern NKVD. He published some material on it in the Japanese periodical *Kaizo* in April 1939.

Lyushkov had been Deputy Head of the NKVD Secret Political Department in Moscow in 1934–1936, and had actually headed the 'investigation' of the Leningrad Terrorist Center. He gives some useful information on Nikolayev, and he makes clear that the case against the other Leningraders was a frame-up. He is also concerned to defend Yagoda against Stalin's accusations of complicity. But the only factual point he touches on is the murder of Borisov. He was in the Leningrad NKVD office when Agranov ordered Borisov to be sent for "questioning" to the Smolny, and says that though he was "puzzled" and wondered if the "accident" in which Borisov died was "framed," he noted that only half an hour's notice was given, and felt that it would probably not have been possible to organize the murder in that time. This is, of course, not an observation but a deduction, and it is by no means a conclusive one.

Moreover, this is the single point on which the Stalinist story in the Bukharin Trial and Khrushchev's public account to the XXII Congress in 1961 are in accord—that Borisov was indeed murdered and that the supposed accident was faked. Lyushkov is, indeed, able to point out that a detail in the Bukharin Trial version is false—that Zaporozhets, not then in Leningrad, could not have been the direct implementer of the Borisov murder.

The interesting point is different—that Lyushkov evidently was not informed about the central plot—presumably on the old principle of confining such information to those who 'need to know'.

What is a little odder is that over the years 1934–1938 Lyushkov seems not to have heard, as had other NKVD defectors, the hints of something fishy about the Kirov case. We are told, as is indeed natural, that NKVD men who knew each other well and were of similar rank spoke to each other a good deal more freely than in other cases (Orlov, p. 153). And Lyushkov was a favorite of Yezhov's and apparently not much trusted in the old NKVD circles—being the only high official of the old operational departments of State Security to survive into 1938. (There is, of course, an alternative explanation: that he was fully, or largely, aware of the facts but concerned to protect both Yagoda and himself as well against any imputation of the murder.)

At any rate, in 1939 we get a hint from another NKVD defector, V. G. Krivitsky, who wrote in his *In Stalin's Secret Service* that no explanation had ever been given why Stalin was satisfied with the "strange action" of the Leningrad NKVD "in releasing Nikolayev when seized with a revolver and a political diary," as recounted in the Bukharin Trial. He noted that in inner circles of the police "the atmosphere surrounding the case was one of special mystery and gloom" with even intimate comrades evading the subject. He once asked Slutsky, Head of the Foreign Department, about the Leningrad NKVD's role. Slutsky replied. "The case is so shady, you understand, that in general it is best not to pry into it. Just keep as far away from it as you can."[4]

Krivitsky adds, though this is only a comment, that it was not easy to decide who killed Kirov, and that "Besides Stalin, there are probably no more than three or four people alive who could solve the Kirov mystery . . . Stalin eventually may become the sole guardian of all the facts in the Kirov affair."

This sort of comment, suspicion, and deduction is to be found over the whole ensuing period. Nicolaevsky, writing under his own name in the New York *New Leader* in 1941, still calls the case "puzzling," but adds that "one thing is certain; the only man who profited by the Kirov assassination was Stalin."[5] In 1945 the defecting diplomat and soldier Alexander Barmine makes the same point, suggesting that Stalin perhaps only had to hint to Yagoda that if Kirov was negligent about not arresting potential terrorists, there was no need to press the issue.[6]

At the same time peripheral details emerged. One labor camp inmate reaching the West, and publishing in 1951, had met a minor figure charged with being a contact man between Nikolayev and the Finns.[7] Another, published the same year, had served in

Kolyma and met one of the Leningrad NKVD men, who was then head of a mine. This former inmate registered his statement that the truth was quite unlike the story published in the press.[8] But it was not until 1954 that we got any full account. First, and most crucial, was Alexander Orlov's *The Secret History of Stalin's Crimes.*

Orlov was one of the NKVD Foreign Department's leading operatives in Western Europe. He held the rank of "Senior Major of State Security," the equivalent of Divisional Commander (i.e., Major General) in the Red Army. Under the name "Nikolski" he had received the Order of Lenin on 3 January 1937. Unlike Lyushkov, he was from the heart of the old NKVD. He had earlier served in the Economic Department of the NKVD, and was the former superior, and close acquaintance, of L. G. Mironov, who was Head of that Department from the early 1930s to 1937. He also, of course, knew Slutsky and Shpigelglas, Head and Deputy Head of the Foreign Department to 1938, and, less well, several of the other leading security figures. There is no doubt about his access to very sensitive areas.

Orlov's book, even more than "The Letter of an Old Bolshevik," was the subject of many objections. It was sensational. It had a fairly lurid title. It was by a defector, and a former NKVD officer. So far, nothing relevant to its authenticity.

And then, it was 'second-hand'. This is, of course, true. But in addition the information was described as NKVD 'corridor gossip'. This was not true—such information was only given between close acquaintances under careful circumstances. A damaging allegation, on the face of it, was that Orlov was not in the USSR for much of the time. But he was there for some of the time, and the information does not need long periods to acquire. Moreover, some of his sources—Slutsky and Shpigelglas—visited him in Western Europe.

Thus, these a priori objections do not amount to much. On the positive side, his sources were precisely the closest to the facts. And his own status is undoubted. And much of his material has since been confirmed. When we actually test what he says on other themes, we find that even when taken as particularly gossipy and unreliable, he turns out to be reliable. For example, Orlov recounts, and has been accused of absurd fantasizing, that Stalin told Lenin's widow Nadezhda Krupskaya that if she made any more trouble the Party would nominate another widow for Lenin, Elena Stasova. Khrushchev, nearly twenty years later, confirmed this in his memoirs[9] (though saying he would not name the Old Bolshevik woman, who was then still living—a hint which made it clear that it was either Stasova or, less probably, Fotieva). Orlov recounts such things as no more than general political gossip. And when he comes to the Kirov case, and the NKVD in general, his information is in his own field.

As we have said, on coming back to the USSR in 1935 Orlov had been told by a colleague, as Krivitsky had been, "the whole affair is so dangerous that it is healthier not to know much about it." However, he soon found that the Leningrad NKVD chiefs had been given high posts in the Siberian gold fields—though getting their precise location wrong (Lenzoloto instead of Kolyma); and that the highest NKVD officials were sending goods to them. He heard the stories of Stalin's disputes with Kirov over 1934. He was long our only source for the story that in 1934 Stalin and Kirov were in dispute over the rations of Leningrad workers—until Khrushchev gave first-hand evidence of the same thing in his memoirs.[10]

Finally, he tells the story of the assassination plot itself. His version is that Stalin organized it through Yagoda, who entrusted Zaporozhets with the operation. Zaporozhets was directly instructed by Stalin "because Zaporozhets would never have taken such an exceptional assignment concerning a member of the Politbureau from Yagoda alone without the sanction of Stalin himself."[11] Though by no means conclusive, this is on the face of it logical and probable. Zaporozhets then found Nikolayev's name in the NKVD files as a potential assassin; and got in touch with Nikolayev through the agent who had denounced him.

Zaporozhets instructed the agent to encourage Nikolayev to make the attempt on Kirov. The agent was told that the NKVD would in fact prevent the assassination. Nikolayev was detained by the guards on his first attempt to enter the Smolny, but was released.

On the actual assassination, Orlov has Borisov in the Smolny,

though not with Kirov, at the moment of the murder, which con-
flicts slightly with other accounts. And he has Zaporozhets conduct the first interrogation while other accounts say that he was
out of Leningrad.

He describes Stalin's interrogation of Nikolayev, with the latter
making it clear that he knew of the NKVD involvement (Orlov is
the first to state this). As to Borisov, he was "secretly liquidated
by order of Stalin."

A good deal more detail is given, most of which is consistent
with or confirmed by later testimony. It will be seen that Orlov
has misunderstood, or been misinformed, on certain details. But
this is quite normal and does not detract from his general reliability. It cannot be said that he has *proved* Stalin's direct involvement, and we shall consider that in the next chapter. But at any
rate a coherent and generally accurate version taking this view
was now before the public.

It is true that the story was 'sensational'. But, as Professor
Adam Ulam has written:

> We who study Soviet affairs have—why try to conceal it—a skele-
> ton in our filing cabinets. To describe this skeleton let me invoke
> a fictitious case of two fictitious characters, X and Y. In his at-
> tempts to learn as much as possible about the Soviet Union X,
> between roughly 1930 and 1950, read nothing but the works of
> reputable non-Communist authors. He grounded himself on the
> writings of the Webbs and Sir John Maynard. Turning to the
> American academicians, he followed the studies of the Soviet
> government, law and various aspects of Soviet society which
> might have come from the pen of a professor at Chicago, Har-
> vard, Columbia or Williams. This serious intellectual fare would
> be supplemented by the reading of the most objective non-
> academic experts on Russia, and finally of those few journalists
> who had no axe to grind, especially the ones who had spent a
> long time in the Soviet Union.
>
> His friend Y had an equal ambition to learn, but his taste ran to
> the non-scholarly and melodramatic. Indifferent to objectivity, he
> would seek the key to Soviet politics in the writings of the avowed
> enemies of the regime, like the ex-Mensheviks; he would delight
> in the fictional accounts à la Koestler or Victor Serge. Sinking

lower, and would pursue trashy or sensational stories of the 'I was a Prisoner of the Red Terror' variety. He would infuriate X by insisting that there were aspects of Soviet politics which are more easily understood by studying the struggle between Al Capone and Dan Torrio than the one between Lenin and Martov, or the dispute about 'socialism in one country'.

Which of our fictitious characters would have been in a better position to understand the nature of Soviet politics under Stalin?[12]

In 1954 another book of reminiscences, in part about the Kirov case, came out—*Face of a Victim,* by Elizabeth Lermolo. It is not possible to identify her. The late Leonard Schapiro, one of the world's leading scholars on Soviet history, told me that her background was quite authentic. But clearly such an assurance cannot carry too much weight. However, she writes that she lived in the small town of Pudozh, northeast of Leningrad, having been exiled as the wife of a former White officer, though uninterested in politics. She claimed to be a neighbor of an aunt of Nikolayev's, and met him several times on visits. Her name was found in Nikolayev's notebook, and as with all those listed she was arrested on the night of 1 December and flown to Leningrad. There her background emerged, and seemed promising in involving Nikolayev with 'Whiteguard' elements. She was interrogated by Agranov, and by Stalin himself. When she proved a poor 'witness' and the direct Whiteguard line was abandoned, she was in prison with other peripheral women in the case, and eventually sent to an 'isolator'.

There is nothing implausible in this. Her memory of her interrogation, recorded a good deal later, is doubtless misapprehended in detail, but not obviously or impossibly so. Her accounts of what she did not observe herself are often wrong. But her description of Nikolayev, and of his wife, mother, and sisters, and of others who were deported in connection with the 'Moscow Center' is credible and on some points confirmed. The difficulty is that we cannot be fully convinced of any of this. It is clear that she had access to true and obscure information, but it is impossible with our present resources to determine the degree to which this has become distorted. Rightly or wrongly, I have been chary of using her evidence, even though it seems to contain a stratum of fact.

So, the position at the beginning of 1956 was that the 1938 official version remained orthodox in the USSR, but that Orlov's account directly implicating Stalin was on record in the West. In
February 1956, however, came Khrushchev's "Secret Speech" to
the XX Congress of the Communist Party of the Soviet Union.
On the Kirov issue he said:

> It must be asserted that to this day the circumstances surrounding
> Kirov's murder hide many things which are inexplicable and mys-
> terious and demand a most careful examination. There are rea-
> sons for the suspicion that the killer of Kirov, Nikolayev, was as-
> sisted by someone from among the people whose duty it was to
> guard Kirov's person. A month and a half before the killing,
> Nikolayev was arrested on the ground of suspicious behavior, but
> he was released and not even searched. It is an unusually suspi-
> cious circumstance that when the Chekist assigned to protect
> Kirov was being brought in for interrogation, on 2 December
> 1934, he was killed in an automobile 'accident' in which no other
> occupants of the car were harmed. After the murder of Kirov,
> top functionaries of the Leningrad NKVD were given very light
> sentences, but in 1937 they were shot. We can assume that they
> were shot in order to cover the traces of the organizers of Kirov's
> killing.

It will be seen that though Khrushchev adds the odd detail, what
he reveals does not differ essentially from the evidence of Yagoda
and Bulanov at the 1938 trial. His comment on the "many things"
which are inexplicable and mysterious and demand a most careful
examination, however, can only mean that the story as presented
at that trial and its predecessors is not the true one.

Khrushchev told the Warsaw First Secretary Stefan Staszewski
in 1956 (though this was not published until 1985, and then unofficially), "The trial of the Kremlin doctors was provoked by
Stalin . . . The death of Kirov was also a provocation, and we
still don't have all the details of his death."[13]

In 1961, at the XXII Congress, Khrushchev spoke (this time
publicly) about the affair:

> The mass repressions began after the murder of Kirov. A great
> deal of effort is still necessary to determine fully who was guilty

of his death. The more deeply we study the materials relating to Kirov's death, the more questions arise. It is noteworthy that Kirov's assassin had previously been twice arrested by the Chekists near the Smolny, and that weapons had been found on him. But both times, upon someone's instructions, he had been released. And this man was in the Smolny, armed, in the very corridor along which Kirov usually passed. And for some reason or other it happened that at the moment of the murder the chief of Kirov's bodyguard had fallen far behind S. M. Kirov, although his instructions forbade him to be so far away from the person he was guarding.

The following fact is also very strange. When the chief of Kirov's bodyguard was being driven to the interrogation—and he was to have been questioned by Stalin, Molotov, and Voroshilov—on the way, as the driver of the vehicle later said, an accident was deliberately staged by those who were to bring the chief of the bodyguard to the interrogation. They reported that the chief of the bodyguard had died in the accident, although actually he had been killed by the persons escorting him.

Thus the man who guarded Kirov was killed. Then those who had killed him were shot. This was apparently not an accident but a premeditated crime. Who could have committed it? A thorough study of this complex case is now under way.

It was found that the driver of the vehicle that was carrying the chief of S. M. Kirov's bodyguard to the interrogation is alive. He has said that as they were riding to the interrogation an NKVD man was sitting with him in the cab. The vehicle was a truck. (It is strange, of course, that this man was being driven to the interrogation in a truck, as if in this case no other vehicle could be found for the purpose. It seems that everything had been thought out in advance, down to the smallest detail.) Two other NKVD men were in the back of the truck with the chief of Kirov's bodyguard.

The driver went on to say that as they were driving down the street the man sitting next to him suddenly grabbed the wheel out of his hands and steered the truck directly at a house. The driver grabbed the steering wheel back and straightened out the truck, and they merely sideswiped the wall of the building. Later he was told that the chief of Kirov's bodyguard had been killed in this accident.

Why was he killed while none of the persons accompanying him was even injured? Why were both these NKVD men who were escorting the chief of Kirov's bodyguard later themselves shot? This means that someone had to have them killed in order to cover up all traces.

Once again, the story was not incompatible with the Yagoda–Bulanov version. And once again Khrushchev implied that the true culprit or culprits had yet to be named. To say that "a great deal of effort is still necessary to determine fully who was guilty of his death" and that "the more deeply we study the materials relating to Kirov's death, the more questions arise" is in effect to repudiate the Stalinist version.

As to Khrushchev's assurance that a study of the case was now under way, it is reported that a Commission of Inquiry was set up in 1956 or 1957. It took a large amount of evidence—200 volumes is the figure mentioned. Hundreds of witnesses were called, and the commission had access to all the secret archives.[14] This was only a little over twenty years after the event. Many who knew a good deal were available. Some refused to testify—Fomin among others. One former NKVD officer is reported saying to an official of the Commission: "Aren't you frightened of involving yourself in such a matter?" Another, a former colleague of Zaporozhets, said, "Why is this necessary for you?" and added, "Aren't you afraid? Automobile accidents can be arranged." He concluded by declaring, "I am saying nothing to you. I want to live."[15]

The Commission went to look at the scene of Borisov's accident, and heard the driver's evidence, and that of doctors who had then had to certify Borisov's death as accidental, but now attributed it to blows of an iron bar.[16]

But none of this was made public, and it is unofficially reported that the Commission's report was simply shelved; but that later, in the 're-Stalinization' which followed Khrushchev's fall, some witnesses were interrogated further with a view to their withdrawing their evidence. . . .[17]

Meanwhile, other developments relevant to the case took place. In 1962 Yenukidze, allegedly the master mind behind Yagoda's orders to Zaporozhets, was fully rehabilitated.[18] And Bukharin and Rykov were, in a rather obscure context, cleared of terrorism.[19]

The treatment of the great trials and the whole Trotskyite conspiracy in Soviet works of reference was remarkable. In the volumes of the first and second edition of the *Large Soviet Encyclopaedia* that appeared up until 1955, the articles on Trotskyism and on the Right Deviation end with descriptions of the trials and characterization of the oppositionists as "a band of spies and murderers."

By August 1956, the party struggle is, in the main, only treated up to about 1930, and, if later, merely to denounce Trotsky's "Fourth International" as a continuation in exile of his factiousness. Similarly, the article on Kirov in 1953 speaks of his murder by "a Trotskyite monster, an agent of imperialist intelligence and a member of the counterrevolutionary Zinovievite underground group, acting on the direct orders of the enemies of the people, Trotsky, Zinoviev and Kamenev." On his next appearance, in 1973, the murderer is merely "an enemy of the Communist Party." Similarly, the 1962 Party history no longer mentions the Zinovievite connection with the assassination.

Thus the trials, and the accusations of responsibility for the Kirov murder, were just abandoned. No public repudiation of the trials took place, and so no clear story about the main political events of the late 1930s existed at all. A strange and anomalous situation.

Another change between the earlier accounts and those given in Khrushchev's time was in the treatment of the period before the murder. It was now revealed that at the XVII Congress there had been a plan to remove Stalin from his post.[20] And that Kirov and other 'moderates' in the Politburo had prevented Stalin taking 'reprisals' against important Communists.[21]

All this was now at least on record. But no clear account of the period, and no clear verdict on the murder, were made public.

While Khrushchev cast doubt, and more than doubt, on the Stalinist explanation, he effectively repeated the accusations against Yagoda, Zaporozhets, and the NKVD. This leaves the charges against the opposition leaders as the dubious element in the Stalinist story. The rehabilitation of Yenukidze meant that Yagoda, unless acting on his own, had received instructions from someone else. But, as we have seen, Khrushchev also said that the Leningrad NKVD officers were, "it is possible," shot to "cover the traces of the organizers of Kirov's killing." At the time of the shooting of these officers Yagoda had been under arrest for months. So it cannot have been he who was now in a position to give orders to "cover the traces." Another authority must have had the motive and the power to do this. The implications are obvious, but they remained implications.

In private, Khrushchev told Tvardovsky that he was certain of Stalin's guilt in the matter.[22] And Stalin's daughter rightly comments on his "transparent hints" that her father was guilty.[23] But he seems never to have been able to secure a public airing of the case.

So even when the main facts seemed to be established, and the earlier suspects openly or implicitly cleared, there was not a definite identification of the guilty. This remained the position to 1988. And, in the meantime, nothing official was published to confirm or add to what had come out in the Khrushchev period. This was clearly the result of a decision at the top level to prevent any further revelations. There is even what may be an odd piece of negative evidence: when Khrushchev's *Memoirs* were sold to the West, reportedly with KGB connivance, they contained no reference to the Kirov murder (though they did recount one of the earlier disputes between Kirov and Stalin).

At any rate, for more than twenty years the story before the Soviet public remained at the point at which Khrushchev had left it.

In the underground world of samizdat, however, much evidence emerged over this period.

In the late 1960s Roy Medvedev produced his great *Let History Judge*. In it he gives details of the attempt to replace Stalin at the XVII Congress and of the voting at that Congress. On the Kirov murder he recounts the Nikolayev–Zaporozhets–Yagoda connection with further information on the arrests and releases of the assassin. He relies on three sources, including I. M. Kulagin who was actually present, for a description of Stalin's interrogation of

Nikolayev, with the point that Nikolayev said that the NKVD had arranged the murder.[24] He tells, again from a party source, E. P. Frolov, then an assistant of Yezhov's, that Yezhov was with Stalin the whole day on 1 December. He quotes Kulagin on Borisov's wife coming to him having escaped from a psychiatric hospital, but dying, apparently poisoned, soon afterwards.

He quotes various witnesses, including Smorodin's daughter, as to minor details, though usually at second- or third-hand. He also cites an NKVD officer, Katsafa, who had been one of Nikolayev's guards in prison. And he tells us that the list of the 'Leningrad Center' and the 'Moscow Center', as drafted by Stalin himself, was available to investigators in the period after the 1956 Party Congress. He concludes that Stalin's guilt appears to be "logically and politically, almost proved."

Shortly afterwards, Peter Yakir, son of the executed Army Commander, in his *A Childhood in Prison* gave a few details. These included an account of the trial of Nikolayev and the 'Leningrad Terrorist Center' given him by A. A. Batner who had been Clerk of the Court, which made it clear that the case was a frame-up. There is also some interesting, though not substantial, information from Yakir's cellmate, the son of Medved; and a few facts from a private conversation with Fomin.

At the end of the 1970s came Anton Antonov-Ovseenko's *The Time of Stalin*. He too describes, with slightly different detail, the conversations about replacing Stalin by Kirov, which took place early in 1934. And (again with some differences, but more fully) the voting at the XVII Congress, obtained from a member of the Control Commission, which examined the papers in 1957. He quotes various named witnesses, including Kirov's Old Bolshevik sister-in-law, testifying to Kirov being in fear of his life in 1934.

Antonov-Ovseenko recounts Nikolayev's difficulties, stating that he had written to Stalin about them and that his reinstatement in the Party was on orders from Moscow. He gives new details about Nikolayev's and Kirov's movements in the Smolny in the evening of the assassination. His account of Stalin's interrogation of Nikolayev differs from Medvedev's in detail, but he too has Nikolayev saying that the NKVD had made him kill Kirov—and had given him "four months of target practice." (His sources are the Provincial Prosecutor Palgov—and Medved, though at second- or third-hand and years later.) He gives a few new details on the Borisov murder. And, like Medvedev, he tells of the NKVD officer Katsafa. His account of the Leningrad Center trial has Nikolayev at first denying the charge but finally being borne down by Ulrikh and confirming his earlier confession.[25] In addition, he gives some details about the Leningrad police officials and their positions in labor camps.

And he says that the commission appointed by Khrushchev had in fact reported, and Khrushchev had promised to make their findings public, but that the decision was reversed.

Much of Medvedev's and Antonov-Ovseenko's material seems to be from witnesses who gave evidence to that Commission. The same seems to be true of our next main source. In 1987 the writer Anatoly Rybakov published in the Soviet press a book he had written years previously—*Children of the Arbat*. Though it is in the form of fiction, and is believed to have been censored on some points, Rybakov himself states flatly, "not a single action by Stalin in the novel is invented, they are all supported by evidence."[26]

Stalin several times, and at considerable length, speaks on Kirov's faults, including his defense of Ryutin and others. He thinks of his dangerous independence in control of Leningrad. And in a typical passage he tells Yagoda that the Leningrad organization is failing to deal with the ex-oppositionists, that Kirov protects them: "Kirov shepherds the Trotskyite snake against Stalin, but won't it bite Kirov itself?" As to the detail of the murder plot, we have recounted in Chapter IV how Rybakov tells of Zaporozhets starting to take orders from Yagoda rather than Medved, and of his bringing in five 'likely lads' from the Moscow NKVD. It does not seem likely that the Soviet censorship would have allowed these factual allegations and details to pass if they were mere inventions.

When it comes to establishing, or rather hinting, the final guilt, Rybakov has a 'good' NKVD officer who hears that Zaporozhets has sent to the central NKVD for these 'lads' in connection with very important duties. He concludes that some 'action' is being planned. His suspicions had already been aroused by Zaporozhets's own appointment earlier.

The NKVD officer finds in the files a letter from Nikolayev, complaining of being removed from his RKI job by 'Trotskyites', and of being sent to work in a factory, where the party secretary, also a 'Trotskyite', sent him on a party mobilization for transport. He was willing to go where the Party sent him; but 'Trotskyites', rather than the Party, had exiled him from Leningrad. So he refused and was expelled from the Party. He had sent twenty letters to Kirov about this alleged Trotskyite penetration of the Leningrad apparatus but had no anwser. This was probably due to the Trotskyites surrounding Kirov, whom Kirov foolishly trusted. Meanwhile, Nikolayev was desperate and "ready for anything." Could this mean a terrorist act? In any case, the NKVD man concludes that Zaporozhets is working with this man. What, then, were Zaporozhets's 'lads' intended for? Stalin, it was obvious, was dissatisfied with Leningrad, and wanted Kirov to institute terror against the former Zinovievites. Since Kirov refused, how could this be done? Zaporozhets must create an incident which would overcome Kirov's resistance. But if there were such an act in Leningrad, Kirov would be in charge of the investigation. So it must be something that would force him to change his mind. A railway sabotage? No. The murder of Chudov, Kodatsky, or Pozern? Would Nikolayev do that? And if he did, Kirov would still be in charge of the investigation. What then? The officer remembers Stalin in 1918 in Tsaritsyn, when it was proposed to shoot some Red Army officers and, on being told that there was a problem in that evidence against them was doubtful, replying "Death solves all problems. No man—no problem." The officer does not pursue this train of thought further; but its trend is obvious.

And if Rybakov *still* does not quite assert Stalin's guilt, some minor Soviet reviewers took it for granted. In a provincial Young Communist paper, for example, one reads that Zaporozhets's "likely lads . . . prepared the murder of Kirov." And more broadly and conclusively: "Stalin's participation in that murder has been talked about before. A. Rybakov for the first time gives that version literary expression, and by artistic means convinces us of its reality"—which is not, of course, to say that the whole story had been told.[27]

Then, in December 1987, the Soviet periodical *Ogonyok* published a section of Anastas Mikoyan's memoirs which had been banned in its earlier editions. In it, as we noted in Chapter IV, he fully confirmed samizdat accounts of the ill-feeling between Stalin and Kirov; of the attempt to replace Stalin with Kirov at the XVII Party Congress; and of Stalin harboring feelings of vengeance against the Congress delegates "and, of course, against Kirov personally."[28]

Until the official Commission's findings are published, it seems unlikely that we will have much more to go on. But, as we have seen, there is a good deal of evidence, and in our next chapter we shall examine it with a view to a full analysis and a true verdict.

CHAPTER XIV

Verdict

That Nikolayev was guilty of the murder of Kirov seems clear. His motives appear to have been personal. The main question is not Nikolayev's guilt, but the way in which he was enabled to carry out the murder.

From what we have seen, Stalin is the obvious suspect. But we may first consider the others implicated over the period 1934–1938.

As an assassination serving political ends, we must first exclude the 'Whiteguards'. Not because any genuine Whiteguards among them (perhaps there were some) might not have been happy to kill any Communist, but because there is no evidence of their doing so, and after a few days it was hardly even suggested. This leaves us with the oppositionists.

After years of exile and repression Zinoviev and Kamenev had just been readmitted to the Party, and had even been allowed to address the Party Congress in February 1934, meeting some minor abuse but, in some cases, even applause. The atmosphere was one of reconciliation, and their future appeared brighter than it had for many years. It is true that they might have thought that the elimination of Stalin would be a good thing. But what is remarkable about the conversations we know of between oppositionists in isolators—and even the letters of Trotsky in exile—is the calculation that Stalin would sooner or later be forced, for political reasons, into some sort of reconciliation. An idea which the recent relaxation could only strengthen.

The assassination of Kirov could only, from their point of view, have the effect which indeed it really did have: terror, further assaults on the opposition and on themselves in particular.

Bukharin and the Rightists, accused of complicity not directly in providing the assassin, but indirectly through the police connection, could have even less reason for such action. They were still in the Party and in the Central Committee. They, even more than the Zinovievites, could hope for further relaxation.

As for the idea of Yagoda operating on his own, there seems to be even less reason to be found. Both Stalinist and non-Stalinist versions reject it, and no plausible motive has ever been alleged.

An autonomous plot by Zaporozhets and a group of local NKVD accomplices has the disadvantages that, first, there is no evidence for it; second, that it, too, is incompatible with both the Stalinist and non-Stalinist versions of his complicity; third, that it does not jibe with the efforts from above to omit Zaporozhets from the police officials first arrested, and later to give him a derisory sentence and protect him thereafter.

That experienced Communists could have thought that the murder of Kirov could accomplish anything seems highly unlikely. But a plot to kill him and Stalin together is, on the face of it, more plausible. In the Indictment in the 1936 trial, indeed, Bakayev is quoted as saying that he had been instructed by Zinoviev "to organize the assassination of Stalin in Moscow and Karev to organize the assassination of Kirov in Leningrad." Zinoviev confirmed this.[1] But this plan against Stalin was not pursued in the text; and all the alleged attempts to get near enough to Stalin to kill him are placed later (and none of them is connected with the Zinovievites).

But an even more weighty point appeared in the 1938 trial. Those denounced as among Yagoda's 'Rightist' plotters and spies included Commissar of State Security Second Class K. V. Pauker and Senior Major A. I. Volovich, Head and Deputy Head of the NKVD Operative Department, and themselves directly and personally responsible for Stalin's own security. Pauker (a former barber) used to shave him. Volovich acted as his driver. Yet this unique access to a prominent victim had not been made use of by the conspirators!

The material given in the Soviet press in the 1950s and 1960s effectively disposes, in fact, of the guilt of all the 'oppositionists' but at the same time makes it clear that elements in the NKVD really were involved. The almost inevitable conclusion is that Nikolayev acted for his own motives, but had his way cleared by Zaporozhets and his men, acting on the orders of Yagoda. As we have said, no plausible motive either for Zaporozhets or for Yagoda to have committed the murder on their own initiative has ever been advanced. Yagoda's alleged supervisor in the plot, Yenukidze, has been cleared. This leaves Stalin's guilt as the only story which is compatible with the evidence.

This is not say that the evidence, circumstantial on the one hand and logical on the other, would necessarily be enough to ensure conviction in a Western court of law. In the same way, David Irving has sought to show that there is an absence of positive evidence for Hitler ordering the Holocaust. But these legal criteria are not the point.

For here we should note an important distinction. In his essay on the trial of Warren Hastings, Macaulay notes that the English courts' "rules of evidence, it is well known, exclude much information which would be quite sufficient to determine the conduct of any reasonable man . . . those rules, at every assizes, save scores of culprits whom judges, jury and spectators firmly believe to be guilty. But when those rules were rigidly applied to offences committed many years before, at a distance of many thousand miles, conviction was, of course, out of the question. . . . But it is clear that an acquittal so obtained cannot be pleaded in bar of the judgement of history."

In historical investigation, evidence is always of variable quality. First-hand evidence may be false. Third-hand evidence may be sound. Witnesses can be compared and their partiality, errors, and incompetence be allowed for in using them in conjunction with others. Speculations, deductions, may be probable, or virtually certain. Circumstantial evidence may be decisive. And, as we have said, the evidence we have scarcely admits any other solution but Stalin's guilt.

Apart from evidence, the first obvious question to be put in all murder cases is, of course, *cui bono*—who benefits? That someone benefits from a murder does not necessarily prove that he did it; but in the absence of any other beneficiaries it is always strong grounds for suspicion.

Here the answer is clear: a subordinate who was giving trouble was removed; and the way was simultaneously opened to the establishment of a full Stalin autocracy. As we have seen, no one among the ex-oppositionists accused of the crime could possibly have benefited in any way; nor have the NKVD operatives we take to have procured the murder ever been alleged to have had any plausible motive of their own. Thus, to the question who was able to use the assassination for his own purposes, the answer we must give is, Stalin.

The next question is, was it in character for Stalin to organize the murder? Or, to put it another way, is it or is it not inherently implausible that he should have done so?

The use of murder of this sort is to be found in later Stalinist acts. As Roy Medvedev tells us, "some officials were murdered in their homes, in hotels, on hunting parties, in their offices, thrown out of windows, poisoned—and were then reported dead of heart attacks, accidents, or suicides."[2]

In a different vein, we have the murder of Trotsky, in 1940. The assassin, Ramon Mercader, was spoken of in Communist circles as a disillusioned Trotskyite; and he served his sentence in a Mexican jail without telling the true story—though going, when released, to Czechoslovakia and (when that country proved unsuitable in 1968) moving to the Soviet Union. In fact, we have clear evidence that the true story is the obvious one. The assassination was planned in Moscow, where three floors of the NKVD Registry were devoted to the Trotsky project. It was supervised by Gaik Ovakimian, Soviet Consul in New York, and later an NKVD Major General, and the active agent N. I. Eitingon (also an NKVD Major General in 1945) was actually on the spot, as was the assassin's mother who returned to the USSR and accepted Mercader's Order of Lenin for him in his absence.

A closer parallel to the Kirov murder, in that it took place in the USSR and was of a man officially held in high repute, took place in 1948. The great Yiddish language actor-producer Solomon Mikhoels was one of the Soviet Union's most prominent Jewish personalities. He had been a leading figure in the Jewish Anti-Fascist Committee, and had visited the United States during the war. At the time of his death he was to all appearances in very good odor with the state. In 1948 it was announced that he had died in an accident in Minsk.

But, as it turned out, his death was the first blow in the anti-Semitic campaign of Stalin's last years. In the next year or so almost all his colleagues were arrested. In 1952 the leading Yiddish writers were shot, in the so-called 'Crimean Affair'. And in January 1953 Mikhoels himself was posthumously branded as a traitor.

His death had been announced as a car accident. After Stalin's death, it was admitted that it had actually been carried out by the Secret Police, under the orders of their Minsk chief, L. F. Tsanava, and it is clear that it was done on Stalin's orders.[3] His precise motives are unknown, presumably including a wish to rid himself of the leading and best-known figure in Soviet Jewry, but not yet to face the political price in the West. At any rate, his motives in the Kirov case are far more straightforward and urgent.

The fate of Kirov's old colleague, and ally in "moderate" opposition, Sergo Ordzhonikidze presents another, and in some ways closer, illustration of Stalin's methods. It was announced on 18 February 1937 that he had died of paralysis of the heart: a medical report signed by the People's Commissar for Health and three other leading doctors appeared in the press.

Rumors soon circulated that it was in fact a case of suicide or murder. And it was noted that most of Ordzhonikidze's subordinates, and a number of his relatives, were shot or disappeared; and, later, that towns called after him were renamed. But he remained formally in high posthumous repute, as an old comrade-in-arms of Stalin's.

Only in 1956, in his "Secret Speech" to the XX Party Congress, and more publicly in 1961 in his report to the XXII Party Congress, did Khrushchev announce that Ordzhonikidze had been driven to suicide. Accounts soon appeared of the last days of his life, with attempts to reason with Stalin, ending in angry exchanges; of the NKVD searching his flat; of the execution after torture of his brother; of his widow telephoning Stalin with the news of his death, and being told that heart attacks were unpredictable; of the Health Commissar's reluctance to sign the medical report. . . .[4]

Suicide remained the official story over the decades that followed, though there was clearly an inconsistency in even Stalin talking to the widow about heart attacks if shooting (as Khrushchev had said) was the method, rather than (say) poison. But in April 1988 a prominent Soviet historian, who had examined Ordzhonikidze's papers and interviewed witnesses, published an article saying that there were various versions of Ordzhonikidze's death, but that he was in an energetic mood, making various appointments for next day and showing no sign whatever of depression.[5] The unstated implication is clearly that it was not a suicide. And, as with Kirov himself, we can presumably expect further investigation. The case differs from Kirov's in that no enemy of Stalin was accused of murder. It resembles it as yet another removal of an obstacle to Stalin's achievement of complete power. Kirov's death marked the beginning of that process. Ordzhonikidze's marked the end, being immediately followed by the February–March 1937 plenum of the Central Committee which launched unlimited tyranny and unlimited terror.

These parallels are not exact, but may all the same be thought relevant—certainly as to whether it was in or out of character for Stalin to have procured Kirov's murder. His motives would be to remove an obstacle to his drive to autocracy, and to provide a reason for terror against others.

What can be said in Stalin's defense?

It was clear to most observers that Stalin's story about the involvement of Zinoviev and Bukharin and the other former leaders in the plot was untrue. But, of course, this did not prove that Stalin himself was responsible. Many believed that the assassination was merely an individual act of which Stalin took advantage. The evidence of police involvement was definite but skimpy, and possibly invented. Even if Zaporozhets was involved, this did not prove even Yagoda's guilt, established only by his confession, perhaps as false as those of Bukharin and the others. Even if Yagoda was guilty, Stalin might not be.

It was not until the 1950s that the first real evidence of Stalin's complicity appeared, and it was naturally unverifiable. Even in the early 1970s a few reputable scholars refused to believe it, mainly on the grounds of the supposed improbability of Stalin doing anything of the sort.

Adam Ulam, worthy of a hearing as one of the most distinguished of American sovietologists, argued that to use Yagoda would have been "a very clumsy and dangerous way to get rid of somebody," since Stalin did not trust Yagoda and could have lost power if Yagoda had told the other Polituro members. He added, "It is unlikely that Stalin would have wanted to establish the precedent of a successful assassination attempt against a high Soviet official," since this would encourage attempts on himself. Ulam dismissed the idea that Kirov led a 'liberal' wing in the Politburo, or had "aroused Stalin's jealousy" as "later reconstructions with no basis in established fact."[6]

It was indeed, up to a point, a clumsy operation, which does not mean it can be dismissed a priori. The question of a 'precedent' is an entirely abstract point—and underestimates Stalin's security arrangements: it had been difficult enough, after all, to penetrate Kirov's. And the fact of Stalin's hostility to Kirov, then deducible, is now proven. Thus Ulam's arguments, though not unreasonable in themselves, are either so general as to carry little weight, or fail on empirical grounds.

Ulam (who has lately written a novel called *The Kirov Affair,* though in fact covering the whole Stalin period) was the only major Western sovietologist to argue on these lines. His case seems to show that even those in no way well affected to Stalin found it hard to understand how far he was prepared to go. Ulam, indeed, only devotes a few paragraphs to this argument, and does not attempt a broad examination of the assassination and its background and circumstances.

As is perhaps only right, while silence on, rather than exculpation of, Stalin prevailed even in the most hard line circles in the Soviet

Union, another Western academic has quite recently argued in detail and at length that there is no sufficient case against Stalin.[7] In the interest of fairness (and having, as it were, presented the case for the prosecution), we should look carefully at this case for the defense.

It states that Trotsky "believed that the assassination was really the work of misguided young oppositionists." This is an error, one that arises from a failure to read all Trotsky wrote on the subject in 1935–1936 (see pp. 58, 71, 104). It also cites Ulam's skepticism of the charge. But it goes on to make a single serious point.

As it notes, Lyushkov, writing in 1939 after his defection, did not know of (or said he did not know of) the NKVD connection. Since he was an investigator of the Leningrad Center, and present at Leningrad NKVD headquarters through the period, this obviously carries weight. However, as we have seen, the only evidence Lyushkov produces for his statement is that Borisov could not have been murdered by the NKVD, since only half an hour or so was given them to organize this event. But since the Borisov murder by NKVD officers was in fact thoroughly authenticated in Khrushchev's time, what this must mean is that Lyushkov was not among the handful of NKVD officers with the 'need to know'. Perhaps Borisov's murder could have been arranged in half an hour, but it could certainly have been prearranged. For Borisov was a witness who would certainly, or probably, have been difficult to avoid calling.

On the actual facts, this defense is concerned to argue first that the murder did not lead directly to the Great Terror of 1937–1938, by which Stalin finally established his unchallenged despotism; second that there is no evidence of any dispute between Kirov and Stalin; and third that Stalin did not procure the murder.

The first words of Evgenia Ginzburg's *Into the Whirlwind,* which we have already quoted, run "The year 1937 really began on the 1st December 1934"—the date of Kirov's death, or, as a recent Soviet article put it, "the murder of Kirov was the overture to 1937"[8]; and most historians agree, though noting that Stalin had to maneuver, in his usual devious way, before the result followed. In this decoupling of the phases, the defense also falls into factual error. It says that the decree of 1 December 1934 on the speedy trial and execution of 'terrorists' was "subsequently rarely used." But it was in fact cited, for example, in the case of Marshal Tukhachevsky in 1937, and in that of Mrs. Ginzburg herself, among others. It seems only to have been the great public trials in which it did not figure (for, of course, these could not be investigated or finished in twenty-four hours without forfeiting their status as major public events).

Then it is denied that there is any reliable evidence of Stalin's being in dispute with Kirov—which if accepted would destroy a *cui bono* on the greater issue of the murder. First, the defense rejects the story (from Bukharin by way of Nicolaevsky) that there was in the early 1930s a "moderate" group in the Politburo, including Kirov, who opposed harsh measures against old party members. It maintains that Kirov was not a "moderate" but a "radical" in economic affairs, as indeed Medvedev also says. This is the merest quibble: the question is whether Kirov was a "moderate" (as Medvedev simultaneously notes) on the question of repressing Bolsheviks. That he was, and that such a "moderate" bloc existed, is confirmed, as we have seen, by all the unofficial sources and also (officially) in *Pravda* as long ago as 17 November 1964.

This already showed the existence of an important dispute between Kirov and Stalin. As we have noted of the XVII Party Congress early in 1934, even official accounts (*Pravda* 7 February 1964 and the *Philosophical Dictionary* 1963, now supported clearly by Politburo member Mikoyan in that part of his *Memoirs* published in 1987) confirm unofficial reports that there was a move to transfer Stalin from the post of General Secretary to one of lesser power; and Kirov was the suggested replacement. It is true that Kirov is reported as rejecting the idea: but obviously (as Mikoyan now tells us) it would hardly leave Stalin other than angered at Kirov's sponsors and at Kirov himself. The assertion that there is no evidence of clashes between Kirov and Stalin was, much earlier, refuted by a first-hand source: Khrushchev, as we saw, writes that he accidentally overheard "an exchange of sharp words" between them (on an issue, Leningrad's ration system, of which moreover we have earlier evidence of disagreement from Orlov).

The defense then maintains that if Yagoda had really organized the crime, it would have been dangerous to let him appear in open dock in 1938. He "knew that he would be shot anyway and it would have been easy for him to let slip that Stalin had put him up to it." There are several objections to this argument. First, it is better to be shot than to be tortured to death, which we are explicitly told was the threat held over the accused. ("The defendants were warned that the tortures would be continued even after the trial if they did not give the necessary testimony."[9]) Second, Yagoda's wife was a hostage to his behavior. Third, the NKVD officers composing the main body of the "public" were ready to interrupt any "provocation" by the accused. Fourth, those who could bring themselves to credit the frame-up would surely have had no difficulty in branding Yagoda as lashing out irresponsibly in a hopeless situation. Moreover (see p. 100), he did even so manage to drop a few hints.

Then it is argued that Khrushchev never said openly that Stalin was responsible, and that he could easily have done so, since he publicly attributed the killing of Postyshev and others to Stalin. But first, Khrushchev's power was *not* complete (as was shown in 1964), and he could not do all he wanted in de-Stalinization. Even the rehabilitation of the generals had to wait a year or more after the XX Congress, in spite of army pressure on his side. The Postyshev comparison is hardly relevant. There had never been any question but that Stalin had ordered Postyshev's execution. This is a quite different matter from a vulgar murder like that of Kirov. In private Khrushchev had said that he had no doubt of Stalin's guilt. But even his public statements that the case contained "many things which are inexplicable and mysterious" and that "the more deeply we study the materials relating to Kirov's death, the more questions arise" are anyhow reasonably decisive. For they clearly dispose of the unsponsored individual assassin, of the story that the Zinovievites were to blame, and of the attribution to Zaporozhets under Yagoda's orders with the (already rehabilitated) Yenukidze as the original begetter. And who does that leave? Indeed, the Commission to investigate the murder which Khrushchev set up never reported after his fall and the beginnings of re-Stalinization. But if Stalin was innocent, why not?

The defense notes that Nikolayev's own motives as given in his diary were personal and that if Stalin and his alleged accomplices had been in full control, they would have suppressed it. We have dealt with this point earlier. And in general, it is true that official reactions were (or appeared) 'confused', but it is traditional that the best laid schemes go awry in one way or another, without this invalidating the idea of a scheme. One has to have a rather abstract view of the way things happen to believe otherwise. There was, as we have said, a certain amount of clumsiness in the execution of the project. On the other hand, it was possible, given Stalin's position, more or less to conceal or mask this. Clausewitz remarks of war that a sound strategy may overcome tactical failures, and over the period which followed, few noted, and fewer were able to publicly remark on, the loose ends and contradictions of the December 1934–January 1935 stories.

The general position of this case for the defense is, however, that accusations against Stalin are usually made by those opposed to Stalin. This is, of course, true in the sense that no pro-Stalinist is likely to make such a charge. The implication that all evidence from anti-Stalinists must be rejected is a convenient one, and not only in this particular context: the same writer tells us that survivors' accounts of the dekulakization and the terror-famine, of the Yezhov terror of the 1930s and the anti-Semitic terror of the 1950s, are unacceptable because of the prejudiced opinions of their authors, which is to say that the evidence of victims against their oppressors can never be believed!

But in general, this defense includes an attempt to justify its attitude by associating all evidence of Stalinist misdeeds with the 'Cold War' or 'McCarthyism': though it extends the same rejection to the evidence or arguments of Nikita Khrushchev, of the 'Leninist' dissident Roy Medvedev, and of such militant Western detente advocates as Professor Stephen F. Cohen.

The defense goes on by pointing out that evidence is 'secondhand' and by referring to Orlov's testimony, for example, as 'dubious'—while also implying a Western political motive for believing such testimony, in that 'before the Cold War no serious authority argued that Stalin was behind the assassination'. One objection to this is that it is untrue: Trotsky did so, for example, as early as 1935, even if a little confusedly. And strong hints, to say the least, were given by, for example, Krivitsky. But in any case the late emergence of an account has no logical bearing on its accuracy.

More important, while it is true that the whole story had not been told officially, so that we have had to rely on indirect evidence, it is totally unhistorical to dismiss such evidence on partisan grounds. If evidence is suspect, this needs demonstrating. A true approach to the whole case, in fact—as with many other investigations of obscure actions—involves careful and critical handling of imperfect and partial witnesses. As it happens, most of those impugned by the defense have been justified, if not always in every detail, by later and independent sources, mainly Soviet.

The ineptness of some of these points in effect leaves little of real substance—what remains is, in fact, the absence of direct proof of Stalin's guilt, as with David Irving's argument on Hitler and the Holocaust. This might carry some weight if the circumstantial evidence were to turn out to be inadequate, or if any other solution were logically compatible with established evidence. But the arguments are worth recording as showing the ability of some Westerners concerned with these and similar matters to abandon even a minimally critical approach. One view of the duties of a defense lawyer would approve this. At any rate, it seems to show that Stalin was justified in his view that his story would be, as he put it, "swallowed" by Westerners. There is, for a variety of reasons—some less disreputable than others—an appetite, still, for deception about the period.

If we take it that Stalin was the main culprit, we still have to establish the mechanism.

That he used Yagoda seems overwhelmingly probable, and that Zaporozhets was the executant seems certain. And Zaporozhets must have had a small number of unidentified accomplices.

How was Zaporozhets brought to consider such a deed?

We are told, as we have noted earlier, that a meeting between Zaporozhets and Stalin could not be avoided.[10] Our source is not accurate as to certain details, and it may be that he has invented this story. But if we consider the probabilities, it is certainly logical, as he says, that Zaporozhets would not have carried out instructions to have a Politburo member murdered without a clear assurance that this was necessary in the higher interests of the Party.

It is easy to see how this might be presented: that Kirov was, either 'objectively' or (perhaps more probably) consciously, acting as an agent of the enemy. In the circumstances, the Party's interests would be harmed if he were brought to trial. So it was necessary to remove him by other means. This use of raison d'état for murder is not, indeed, unique to Stalinism, and similar things may be found in the history of other despotisms. And as to secret agents of the enemy, after all a provocateur, the notorious Malinovsky, had been detected in Lenin's select prerevolutionary Central Committee, smaller than the 1934 Politburo.

On the evidence we have, and the probabilities of the case, it seems that Zaporozhets had a number of accomplices, mainly perhaps supplied by the central NKVD, as has been suggested. As we saw in Chapter XI, the verdict in the case of the "Bloc of Rights and Trotskyites" spoke of Yagoda's "accomplices [plural] working in the Leningrad administration of the NKVD." We are told definitely by Roy Medvedev that Zaporozhets "and other officials of the Leningrad NKVD" were "active participants in the plot."[11] Zaporozhets, after taking his instructions, seems to have looked in the files of the Leningrad NKVD for possible assassins, and was attracted to the idea of Nikolayev.

Though Moscow may already have been interested in Nikolayev, as head of Leningrad State Security Zaporozhets almost certainly got his detailed information on, and later contact with, the potential assassin from the local Secret Political Department; and transmitted orders to remove the Smolny guards through the local Operative Department. The number of his accomplices and the extent of their guilt is as yet unknown. But Zaporozhets's absence from Leningrad when the fatal shot was fired in any case indicates clearly that other officers must have been involved in the plot.

We should, however, just note one report of uncertain reliability, which if true would be a real addition to the story. This is supposedly from a conversation many years later with Stalin's secretary Poskrebyshev (one of the few almost certainly in the know).[12] He is quoted as saying that the fatal shot was in fact fired by a "recruit" from the Leningrad NKVD called Gorlikov. It would certainly have been sensible to have provided a backup in case Nikolayev somehow failed. We have no adequate reason to accept the report as authentically from Poskrebyshev. But a point that tells a little in favor of the story is that it is not made anything of in the article in question, and that there seems little reason to invent it. As against that, we might consider the difficulty—though not impossibility—of 'Gorlikov' concealing himself. At any rate this account (rather like the plot of *The Man who Shot Liberty Valance*) seems worth registering, if only with a view to seeing if it is or is not confirmed in some later Soviet investigation.

Certainly the three NKVD men who killed Borisov were involved in the conspiracy in one way or another. They are in fact described as "members of Stalin's own bodyguard"—that is, of the central Operative Department—Volovich's men. But of course, these killers *may* have been briefed only for this particular murder, and been unaware of the major plot.

If Bal'tsevich was indeed "responsible for the guard service at the Smolny,"[13] and so head of (or an official of) the Leningrad Operative Department, he must have been implicated in Zaporozhets's plot; or at least have transmitted orders to remove the guard.

It is not much to our purpose to discover the guilt, if any, of Fomin and Medved. But Fomin later wrote some unrevealing memoirs about his early Cheka career, which must imply that he was rehabilitated, and therefore presumably innocent of any serious involvement in the crime.

We do not know quite what to make of Medved. Almost all (but not all) sources hold that he was not, or does not seem to be, involved. But we know little of him, apart from his reported friendship with Kirov, to suggest that he was incapable of ruthless acts. Perhaps this one was, or others thought it was, too ruthless for him. On the other hand, after the releases of Nikolayev, and the suspicions then aroused in at least some NKVD minds, it seems unlikely that Medved could have remained wholly unaware that something fishy was going on. Even given the careful avoidance of too much knowledge of or interference in security plans, which already characterized NKVD personnel, all this aroused suspicion among NKVD officers who were not so close to things. Still, on all the evidence available at present, Medved seems not guilty.

Voroshilov also acted in a way incompatible with complicity. It even seems to be the case that Lyushkov, deputy head of the central Secret Political Department, charged with establishing the Zinoviev connection, was unaware of the local NKVD involvement.

On the face of it, then, apart from Stalin, those fully informed of the plot seem to have included Yagoda, Yezhov, Poskrebyshev, almost certainly Agranov, and in Leningrad Zaporozhets and a handful of his trusted men: Bal'tsevich? Kotomin? Gubin? . . .

We have asked earlier why, if the report of the Commission set up by Khrushchev cleared Stalin, it was not published? But meanwhile, in November 1987, a new commission on Stalin's crimes has been announced by Gorbachev. The Kirov case was not specifically referred to. But, in the new style of Soviet journals skirmishing a long way ahead of official statements, we have already noted A. Rybakov's fictional account. Journalism has also been on, and even beyond, the verge of direct allegation. As we saw, one review of Rybakov's book spoke flatly of "Stalin's participation in this murder."[14]

A speaker in a debate on films reported in *Sovietskaya Rossiya* in the summer of 1987 has a curious phrase, "we need true representations of historical figures undeservedly forgotten, of Kirov, Blyukher, Yakir, and many others." To speak of Kirov, after whom towns and theatres and so forth are named by the dozen, as "forgotten" is anomalous. To link him with the slaughtered generals is remarkable, and was done again, even more strikingly, by *Literaturnaya Gazeta* at the end of the year: "Kirov, Tukhachevsky, Yakir, and other innocent victims."[15]

As I write in 1988, a strong effort is being made by the more honest Soviet historians to bring out the truth of the past, and unofficial speakers, even Soviet academics visiting the West, have accepted Stalin's guilt. A Soviet official writes: "Bukharin, Y. Rudzutak, A. Rykov, as well as S. Kirov, fell victim to this struggle. They were removed by Stalin."[16]

At a (nonpublic) meeting in the Central Home of Literature, Igor Engelhart, one of the main speakers, said of the Kirov murder: "To whose advantage was it? It was a provocation in just his style! . . . The investigation into the circumstances of Kirov's murder under Khrushchev was not published. Why not?" The writer Vladimir Sokolov made the same point.[17] An article in a Soviet periodical goes as far as to say "Stalin, sorrowing at his grave, apparently knew well by whom, and why, and how his closest companion-in-arms was destroyed."[18] The Moscow press reports, too, a film sequence where Stalin is shown symbolically raising a rifle with telescopic sights in the direction of Kirov. The reviewer, it is true, still says that this is a false suggestion, since the shot that killed Kirov really came from "a weapon used by the opposition, blind with envy at such genuine human beauty, and fearing it."[19] In Mikhail Shatrov's play *Further . . . Further . . . Further,* produced in Moscow early in 1988, Stalin is dramatically accused of the murder. Shatrov remarked later, "Blows from literature are not enough. Facts are needed." And the historian Yuri Afanasiev noted how odd it was that literary men were now "the pioneers in opening history. . . . If we had a good, well-developed historical science, there would be no job for Shatrov."[20]

These instances show that as late as the early months of 1988 the full truth about Stalin's responsibility, now almost (but not quite) undeniable, had still not been officially registered, though we may be certain that no publication of matter even tending to prove his guilt would be permitted in the USSR if he was, in fact, innocent.

The question of giving at least the central truth of the Kirov murder seems to have been closely connected with the drive to rehabilitate Bukharin. In the latter half of 1987 Bukharin was indeed given long and powerful encomia, and virtual assertions of innocence, in the Soviet press. The legal position was more complex. For any such rehabilitation meant a judicial review of the whole case of the "Bloc of Rights and Trotskyites." But among the defendants was Yagoda, and among the charges was that he had organized the Kirov murder. In February 1988, in a brief and otherwise uninformative statement, all the accused were judicially rehabilitated—with the exception of Yagoda, whose name had simply not been submitted to the judicial commission.[21] But a leading Soviet jurist, commenting on this in a government organ, said that Yagoda had been "one of the central figures in the organization of the murder of S. M. Kirov"; less publicly, at a meeting whose proceedings were *not* officially printed, a spokesman for the prosecutor's office said that they had "objective proof" of Yagoda's responsibility for the Kirov murder. Asked about Stalin's role, he said he preferred not to speculate.[22]

Thus, the open accusation of Stalin's guilt has trembled on the lips of Soviet official spokesmen, and has even been spoken of in scattered references.

Unless there is a sudden political reverse such as aborted the truth in 1964, it seems that Stalin's guilt is on the point of official admission. How long it will then take for the whole story, in all its intricacy, to be made public, is another matter. When it is, there will be much more to add to what appears in this book. Some details will no doubt be shown as differing in one degree or another from the reports we already have. What appears here is detective work on a wide variety of evidence, but not on all that must exist. Yet it will be very surprising if the final verdict differs in any important respect.

Thus we can see that the Kirov case has not only been a crux in the establishment of the Stalin autocracy. It was also, over the period 1956–1988, a crucial issue in the attempt in the USSR to face the truth of the Stalin epoch. It was with the utmost difficulty, like some impacted wisdom tooth, that the real story was extracted. And so it played a new role as the crux, the turning point, in the emergence of a new Soviet attitude to the realities of the past.

It is easy to see why it is especially difficult for the Party to swallow. It has to admit that its former leader not merely killed opponents, but procured a vulgar murder and blamed others. It is a matter not only of terror and treachery but also of hypocrisy.

The editor of the Soviet mass-circulation *Ogonyok* lately said in an interview that when it came to the Stalin terror, "it is not easy yet [i.e., in November 1987] for Gorbachev to say more. When you talk about millions of victims you have to find out who killed them . . . the conservatives are very strong. If he spells out millions he'll have all these people against him."[23]

Yet even the killing of millions can be (and has been) justified on grounds of high policy. When it comes to the underhand murder of a colleague against whom nothing was ever alleged, we are on nastier ground.

There is another character aspect we have not touched on. When Stalin saw Kirov's body lying-in-state, he was so overcome by emotion that he kissed his dead colleague. This may remind us that Zinoviev had sent an obituary of Kirov to *Pravda* early in December 1934, though it was not published. In August 1936 Vyshinsky quoted it in court. Its talk that "the grief of the Party is the grief of the whole people, of all the peoples of the USSR" was, he said, a piece of vile hypocrisy. "The miscreant, the murderer mourns over his victim! Has anything like it ever occurred before? What can one say, what words can one use to describe the utter baseness and loathsomeness of this? Sacrilege! Perfidy! Duplicity! Cunning!"[24] At the January 1937 trial he said that Pyatakov too had "sobbed over the corpse of Kirov whom he had killed," and characterized this as "extreme, literally infinite, moral degradation."[25] Zinoviev, Pyatakov, and the others were rehabilitated in June 1988.

Vyshinsky's charges, transferred from the innocent Zinoviev and Pyatakov to the guilty Stalin, may indeed seem to have a certain appropriateness.

If the Kirov case is the key to the Soviet thirties, it is also, in a different sense, the key to the Soviet eighties. As the truth is flatly and finally told in Moscow, then we can really think in terms of the beginning of a true abreaction of Stalinism.

There are many black deeds to be found in that epoch, from the slaughter of the peasantry to the decimation of the intellectuals, but none which so uniquely combines ruthlessness, treachery, and falsehood. A recent Soviet article characterizes "the logic of Stalin's actions" over the period as "a desperate struggle to secure personal power and then to hold on to it at any cost after the catastrophic failures of 1929–1933, when even the 'leader' himself probably saw his replacement as inevitable. A wily and merciless struggle using the entire arsenal of cunning and perfidy."[26]

Notes

Chapter I. The Murder

1. S. Krasnikov, *Sergei Mironovich Kirov* (Moscow, 1964), p. 143.
2. Krasnikov, p. 200.
3. Ibid.
4. Anton Antonov-Ovseenko, *The Time of Stalin* (New York, 1981), p. 92. (Unless otherwise stated, "Antonov-Ovseenko" henceforth refers to this work.)
5. Antonov-Ovseenko, p. 91.
6. Ibid.
7. Antonov-Ovseenko, p. 92.
8. *Pravda,* 4 December 1934.
9. Ibid.
10. Krasnikov, p. 200; *Pravda,* 4 December 1934.
11. Antonov-Ovseenko, p. 94; *Novoe Russkoye Slovo,* 22 June 1982; Elizabeth Lermolo, *Face of a Victim* (London, 1956), p. 113.
12. *Pravda,* 4 December 1934.
13. Ibid.
14. *The Crime of the Zinoviev Opposition* (Moscow–Leningrad, 1935), p. 18. In the case of quotations from this and other material published in Moscow in English editions, we have Americanized the spelling.

Chapter II. The Assassin

1. *Pravda,* 3 December 1934.
2. Lermolo, p. 56–59.
3. Antonov-Ovseenko, p. 87; Lermolo, p. 15.
4. Lermolo, pp. 15–18.
5. Antonov-Ovseenko, p. 87.
6. Ibid.
7. Lermolo, p. 47; Antonov-Ovseenko, p. 88; *Pravda* 3 December 1934.
8. Lermolo, p. 47; Antonov-Ovseenko, pp. 88–89.
9. Antonov-Ovseenko, p. 88; *Pravda,* 22 December 1934; *The Crime of the Zinoviev Opposition,* p. 23.
10. Boris Nicolaevsky, *Power and the Soviet Elite* (New York, 1965), p. 40; Antonov-Ovseenko, p. 91.
11. G. S. Lyushkov in *Kaizo,* April 1939.
12. Anton Ciliga, *The Russian Enigma* (London, 1940), p. 74.
13. Lermolo, pp. 55–57; *The Crime of the Zinoviev Opposition,* pp. 13–14, 20–21, 49–50; with variations Antonov-Ovseenko, p. 100.
14. Loy W. Henderson, *A Question of Trust* (Stanford, 1980), p. 430.
15. E.g., Henderson, p. 430; Lidiya Shatunovskaya, *Zhizn' v kremle* (New York, 1982), pp. 175–78; Mikhail Haifetz in *Vremya i my* No. 70, 1983, p. 187.
16. Lermolo, pp. 83–84.
17. Roy Medvedev, *Let History Judge* (New York, 1971) [henceforth, unless otherwise stated, "Medvedev" refers to this book], p. 158 (the word translated as "envy" should be "jealousy"); Antonov-Ovseenko, p. 97.
18. Shatunovskaya, p. 175; also see Antonov-Ovseenko, p. 88.
19. Lermolo, p. 80.
20. *The Crime of the Zinoviev Opposition,* p. 19.
21. *Kaizo,* April 1939.
22. Alexander Orlov, *The Secret History of Stalin's Crimes* (London, 1954), p. 31; Antonov-Ovseenko, p. 91.
23. *The Crime of the Zinoviev Opposition,* p. 14.
24. *Report of the Court Proceedings in the Case of the Anti-Soviet "Bloc of Rights and Trotskyites,"* English Edition (Moscow, 1938) [Henceforth *"Bloc of Rights and Trotskyites"*], pp. 558, 572; Speech of N. S. Khrushchev to the XXII Party Congress, 1961; Medvedev, pp. 158–59; Antonov-Ovseenko, p. 91; Orlov, p. 31.

Chapter III. Kirov the Bolshevik

1. Krasnikov, p. 18.

2. Krasnikov, pp. 26–27; S. S. Sinelnikov, *Kirov* (Moscow, 1964), pp. 72–81.

3. Krasnikov, pp. 20–41.

4. A. K. Dolunts, *Kirov na severnom Kavkaze* (Moscow, 1973), pp. 18, 21, 25, 48, 75; Krasnikov, p. 43ff.

5. V. I. Lenin, *Polnoe sobranie sochinenii,* 5th Ed. (Moscow, 1965–75), 45:20.

6. P. Silin, "Astrakhanskie rastrely," in *Cheka* (Berlin, 1922); *Astrakhanskii front grazhdanskoi voini i S. M. Kirov* (Stalingrad, 1937), p. 27.

7. *Who Was Who in the Soviet Union* (Metuchen, 1972).

8. I. Dubinsky-Rukhadze, *Ordzhonikidze* (Moscow, 1967), p. 266; S. S. Sinel'nikov, *Sto stranits o Sergei Kirove* (Leningrad, 1968), pp. 62–67.

9. *Nash Mironich* (Leningrad, 1969)), p. 43.

10. *Ocherki istorii kommunisticheskoi partii Gruzii* (Tbilisi, 1971), p. 384.

11. *Pravda,* 4 December 1934.

12. Stephen F. Cohen, *Bukharin and the Bolshevik Revolution* (New York, 1973), p. 289.

13. Ciliga, pp. 48–49.

14. Cohen, p. 460, n. 247.

15. Cohen, p. 459, citing *Vestnik Leningradskogo Universiteta,* No. 8, 1968, pp. 82–83; *Istoricheskii arkhiv,* No. 5, 1961, p. 104.

16. Cohen, p. 328.

17. S. M. Kirov, *Izbranniye statii i rechi* (Moscow, 1957), 2:539.

18. I. V. Stalin, *Sochinenii* (Moscow, 1946–1955), 12:11–20, 30–41.

19. Cohen, p. 454, n. 192.

Chapter IV. Kirov and Stalin 1932–1934

1. Sinel'nikov, *Kirov* (Moscow, 1964), p. 214.

2. Alexander Barmine, *One Who Survived* (New York, 1945), pp. 101–102.

3. *Byuleten oppozitsii,* No. 30, quoted in Isaac Deutscher, *Stalin: A Political Biography* (London, 1949), p. 352.

4. Nicolaevsky, pp. 30, 72; Anatoly Rybakov, "Deti Arbata,"

Druzhba narodov, No. 6, 1987, p. 52; Barmine, p. 247. *Literaturnaya gazeta,* 29 June 1988.

5. *Ocherki komunisticheskoi partii Gruzii,* p. 384.

6. *Pravda,* 17 November 1964.

7. *All-Union Conference on Measures to Improve the Training of Scientific-Pedagogical Cadres in the Historical Sciences* (Moscow, 1964), p. 291.

8. *Druzhba narodov,* No. 6, 1987, p. 52. This is rejected by a note in another Soviet publication (*Izvestiia,* 17 August 1987), not on evidential grounds but on the argument that repressions within the party were not then taking place; but the report implies that it was precisely because of Kirov and his supporters that this was so. And see note 4.

9. *Pravda,* 26 May 1964.

10. Nicolaevsky, p. 75.

11. Ibid.

12. Roy Medvedev, *On Stalin and Stalinism* (Oxford, 1979), p. 94.

13. Nicolaevsky, p. 30.

14. Ciliga, pp. 119–20.

15. Ibid., p. 74.

16. V. K. Zavalishin, Manuscript in Nicolaevsky Collection, Hoover Institution Archives, Stanford, California.

17. See Cohen, pp. 353–54.

18. Roy Medvedev, *Nikolai Bukharin* (New York, 1980), p. 96.

19. Zavalishin MS.

20. Nicolaevsky, p. 44.

21. Berger, p. 41.

22. Zavalishin MS.; Nicolaevsky, p. 50.

23. Zavalishin MS.

24. Zavalishin MS.

25. *Druzhba narodov,* No. 6, 1987, p. 89.

26. *Druzhba narodov,* No. 6, 1987, p. 90.

27. *Druzhba narodov,* No. 6, 1987, pp. 89–122.

28. Sinelnikov, *Kirov,* p. 310.

29. *Sotsialisticheskii vestnik,* No. 8, 1934.

30. Mevedev, p. 165; Antonov-Ovseenko, p. 87.

31. *Izvestiia,* 1 December 1939.

32. Zavalishin MS.

33. Nicolaevsky, p. 83.

34. Zavalishin, MS.

35. Krasnikov, pp. 144–45; *Istoriya SSSR* 2nd Edition, (Moscow, 1962), p. 486.

36. Medvedev, pp. 155ff; Antonov-Ovseenko, pp. 80ff.

37. *Astrakhanskiy front*, pp. 5–7.

38. *Pravda*, 2 December 1934.

39. Medvedev, p. 156; Antonov-Ovseenko, p. 80.

40. Antonov-Ovseenko, p. 85.

41. *Pravda*, 7 February 1964.

42. Antonov-Ovseenko, p. 85.

43. Antonov-Ovseenko, pp. 80ff; Medvedev, p. 143.

44. Antonov-Ovseenko, p. 82.

45. N. S. Khrushchev, *Khrushchev Remembers* (New York, 1970), p. 49.

46. N. S. Khrushchev, Secret Speech.

47. *Pravda*, 7 February 1964.

48. *Ogonek*, 13 December 1987.

49. *Druzhba narodov*, No. 6, 1987, p. 122.

50. Krasnikov, p. 196.

51. Medvedev, *Nikolai Bukharin*, p. 96.

52. Such as Jonathan Haslam and Francesco Benvenuti.

53. Valentin Bcrezhkov interviewed in *Sovetskaya molodezh* (Riga), 20 August 1987.

54. F. Benvenuti, "Kirov nella Politica Sovietica," *Annali dell'Instituto per gli Studi Storici* 4 (1973–1975):344–58.

55. Zavalishin MS.

56. Orlov, p. 25.

57. Leningrad secretary in charge of supplies (and described by Khrushchev as a Latvian).

58. *Khrushchev Remembers*, p. 61.

59. *Ogonek*, No. 50, 1987; Medvedev, p. 157.

60. Zavalishin MS.

61. Ibid.

62. Ibid.; *Ogonek*, No. 50, 1987.

63. Nicolaevsky, pp. 47–48.

64. Joseph Berger, *Shipwreck of a Generation* (London, 1971), p. 41.

65. Krasnikov, p. 196.

66. *Voprosi istorii kommunisticheskoi partii Kazakhstana*, No. 6, 1987, 1968, p. 283.

67. Antonov-Ovseenko, p. 84; Medvedev, p. 158.

68. *Druzhba narodov*, No. 6, 1987, p. 140.

69. *Druzhba narodov*, No. 6, 1987, pp. 140–41.

70. *Druzhba narodov*, No. 6, 1987, p. 141.

71. Antonov-Ovseenko, pp. 85–86.
72. *Pravda,* 29 November 1934.
73. Nicolaevsky, p. 22.

Chapter V. Stalin Interrogates

1. Henderson, p. 428.
2. Khrushchev, Secret Speech.
3. *Pravda,* 4 December 1934.
4. Medvedev, p. 159.
5. Medvedev, p. 160.
6. Antonov-Ovseenko, p. 92.
7. *Kaizo,* April 1939; Orlov, p. 35.
8. Zavalishin MS.
9. Antonov-Ovseenko, p. 90; *Druzhba narodov,* No. 6, 1987.
10. Antonov-Ovseenko, p. 90.
11. *Stenographic Report of the XVII Party Congress.*
12. Antonov-Ovseenko, p. 90.
13. *Druzhba narodov,* No. 6, 1987; Orlov, p. 29.
14. Antonov-Ovseenko, p. 90; Orlov, p. 29.
15. Orlov, pp. 30–31.
16. Medvedev, p. 159; Antonov-Ovseenko, p. 91.
17. Peter Yakir, *A Childhood in Prison* (London, 1972), pp. 93–94.
18. *Pravda,* 26 January 1935.
19. *The Crime of the Zinoviev Opposition,* p. 19.
20. Ibid.
21. Orlov, pp. 33–34.
22. Orlov, p. 34; Antonov-Ovseenko, p. 93; Medvedev, p. 159.
23. *The Crime of the Zinoviev Opposition,* p. 19.
24. *Kaizo,* April 1939.
25. *S. M. Kirov v Leningrade* (Leningrad, 1966), p. 146.
26. Orlov, p. 35; Medvedev, p. 59; Antonov-Ovseenko, p. 93.
27. Orlov, p. 35; Lermolo, p. 264.
28. See note 22; also Yakir, p. 94.
29. Lermolo, Chapter 2.
30. Nicolaevsky, p. 38.
31. *Kaizo,* April 1939.
32. Antonov-Ovseenko, p. 94.
33. Medvedev, p. 159; Khrushchev, Speech to the XXII Party Congress.
34. Medvedev, p. 159; Antonov-Ovseenko, p. 94.

35. Khrushchev, Speech to the XXII Party Congress.
36. *Kaizo,* April 1939.
37. Yakir, p. 93.
38. *Pravda,* 4 December 1934.
39. Anton Antonov-Ovseenko, *Portret tirana* (New York, 1980), p. 135. This is mistranslated in the English edition (p. 101).
40. V. Petrov, *It Happens in Russia* (London, 1951), p. 162.
41. Nicolaevsky, p. 53.
42. *Pravda,* 4 December 1934.
43. Petrov, p. 27.
44. Yakir, p. 93; see also Orlov, p. 96.
45. *Kaizo,* April 1939.
46. Nicolaevsky, pp. 51–52.

Chapter VI. The First Victims

1. *Pravda,* 4 December 1934.
2. *Pravda,* 6 December 1934, etc.
3. Orlov, p. 19.
4. Sidney and Beatrice Webb, *Soviet Communism: A New Civilization,* 2nd Ed. (London, 1937), p. 1156.
5. Henderson, p. 430.
6. Lermolo, pp. 151–52.
7. See Robert Conquest, *The Harvest of Sorrow* (New York, 1986), Chapters 11, 13.
8. Hrihory Kostiuk, *Stalinist Rule in the Ukraine* (Munich, 1960), pp. 98ff.
9. S. Pidhainy, ed., *The Black Deeds of the Kremlin* (Toronto, 1953), 1:366; Kostiuk, p. 100.
10. Pidhainy, 1:366.
11. *Literaturnaya gazeta,* 5 March 1963.
12. Pidhainy, 1:381; Kostiuk, p. 101.
13. Pidhainy, 1:350.
14. Pidhainy, 1:378–79.
15. *Kratkaya literaturnaya entsiklopediya,* 2nd Ed.
16. Pidhainy, 1:378.
17. Ibid.
18. *Pravda,* 10 June 1935.

Chapter VII. The First Story

1. *Kaizo,* April 1939.
2. Medvedev, pp. 125ff.
3. *Kaizo,* April 1939.
4. Medvedev, p. 157.
5. *The Crime of the Zinoviev Opposition,* p. 5; *Pravda,* 22 December 1934.
6. *The Crime of the Zinoviev Opposition,* pp. 8–20.
7. *Kaizo,* April 1939.
8. *The Crime of the Zinoviev Opposition,* p. 24.
9. *Kaizo,* April 1939.
10. Nicolaevsky, p. 50.
11. *Kaizo,* April 1939.
12. Ibid.
13. Medvedev, p. 164; Antonov-Ovscenko, p. 95.
14. Medvedev, p. 163; and see Chapter IV of the present book.
15. *The Crime of the Zinoviev Opposition,* p. 6.
16. Medvedev, p. 163.
17. *Report of Court Proceedings: The Case of the Trotskyiste-Zinovievite Terrorist Centre,* English Edition (Moscow, 1936) [Henceforth cited as *Trotskyite-Zinovievite Terrorist Centre*], p. 34.
18. Nicolaevsky, p. 51.
19. Berger, p. 161; see also *The Crime of the Zinoviev Opposition,* p. 8.
20. *The Crime of the Zinoviev Opposition,* p. 20.
21. Ibid., p. 19.
22. Ibid., pp. 9–10.
23. Ibid., p. 15.
24. Ibid., p. 8.
25. Nicolaevsky, p. 50.
26. *Proceedings of the VII Congress of the Komsomol* (Moscow, 1926), p. 108.
27. *Alexander Kosarev* (Moscow, 1963), pp. 9–11.
28. *Komsomolskaya pravda,* 23 December 1934.
29. *The Crime of the Zinoviev Opposition,* p. 11.
30. *Pravda,* 18 December 1934.
31. *Pravda,* 16 December 1934.
32. *Pravda,* 17 December 1934.
33. *Pravda,* 22 December 1934.
34. *Pravda,* 23 December 1934.

35. Medvedev, p. 164; *Trotskyite-Zinovievite Terrorist Centre*, p. 136.

36. *Trotskyite-Zinovievite Terrorist Centre*, p. 74.

37. *The Crime of the Zinoviev Opposition*, p. 6; *Pravda*, 23 December 1934.

38. *Bloc of Rights and Trotskyites*, pp. 556–57.

39. Ibid., p. 557.

40. *Pravda*, 23 December 1934.

41. *Ocherki istorii Leningrada* (Moscow-Leningrad, 1964), 2:150.

42. *Pravda*, 23 December 1934.

43. *Pravda*, 26 December 1934.

44. Zavalishin MS.

45. Ibid.

46. *The Crime of the Zinoviev Opposition*, p. 9.

47. Ibid., pp. 11–12.

48. Ibid., p. 14.

49. Henderson, p. 430.

50. *The Crime of the Zinoviev Opposition*, p. 15.

51. Ibid., pp. 20–21.

52. Ibid., pp. 13–14.

53. Ibid., p. 14.

54. Ibid., p. 22.

55. Ibid., pp. 22–23.

56. Ibid., p. 25.

57. Antonov-Ovseenko, pp. 98–100.

58. Yakir, p. 44.

59. Antonov-Ovseenko, p. 100.

60. Berger, pp. 161–62; Roy Medvedev, *On Stalin and Stalinism* (Oxford, 1979), p. 98.

61. Antonov-Ovseenko, p. 100.

62. Ibid.

63. *Byuleten oppositsii*, No. 42, February 1935.

Chapter VIII. The Second Story

1. *The Crime of the Zinoviev Opposition*, p. 33.

2. Ibid., p. 12.

3. Ibid., p. 27.

4. Ibid., pp. 33, 37; Lermolo, p. 94.

5. Ibid., p. 35.
6. Ibid., pp. 33–34.
7. Ibid., pp. 42–44.
8. Ibid., p. 36.
9. Ibid., p. 42.
10. Ibid., p. 36.
11. Ibid., p. 42.
12. Ibid.
13. Ibid., p. 52.
14. Ibid., p. 36.
15. Ibid., p. 39.
16. Ibid., p. 36.
17. *Trotskyite-Zinovievite Terrorist Centre*, p. 145.
18. Ibid., pp. 145–46.
19. *The Crime of the Zinoviev Opposition*, p. 38.
20. Ibid., p. 41.
21. Ibid., pp. 41. 47.
22. Ibid., p. 41.
23. *Pravda*, 17 January 1935.
24. *Pravda*, 16 January 1935.
25. *Trotskyite-Zinovievite Terrorist Centre*, pp. 147–48.
26. Ibid., p. 143.
27. Ibid., pp. 143–45.
28. Ibid., p. 147.
29. *Pravda*, 17 January 1935.
30. E.g., *Pravda*, 17 January 1935.
31. Nicolaevsky, p. 56.
32. *The Crime of the Zinoviev Opposition*, pp. 49–50.
33. Lermolo, p. 56.
34. Robert Conquest, *The Great Terror* (New York, 1973), p. 207.
35. Lermolo, p. 70.
36. Shatunovskaya, p. 172.
37. Antonov-Ovseenko, p. 94.
38. Henderson, p. 431; Barmine, p. 250; Yakir, p. 29.
39. F. O. 371. N1868:6.35.
40. Petrov, Chapter 1.
41. Petrov, p. 49.
42. Ibid.
43. Medvedev, p. 165.

Chapter IX. The Police Connection

1. Yakir, p. 97.
2. *Pravda,* 24 January 1935.
3. Orlov, p. 37.
4. Orlov, pp. 33–34; see also Antonov-Ovseenko, p. 90.
5. Antonov-Ovseenko, p. 91.
6. Henderson, p. 429.
7. Orlov, p. 30.
8. Orlov, p. 20.
9. Nicolaevsky, p. 53.
10. Zavalishin MS.
11. Ibid.
12. *Vremya i my,* No. 70, 1983, p. 187.
13. *Bloc of Rights and Trotskyites,* p. 559.
14. Orlov, p. 22.
15. Victor Kravchenko, *I Chose Justice* (London, 1951), pp. 260–63.
16. Nicolaevsky Archives, Series 178:233/14.
17. Petrov, pp. 125, 162; Kravchenko, p. 270.
18. Antonov-Ovseenko, p. 101.
19. Orlov, p. 22.
20. Nicolaevsky Archives, Series 178:233/14.
21. Ibid.
22. Petrov, p. 143.
23. Petrov, p. 125.
24. Petrov, p. 159; Kravchenko, p. 270.
25. Petrov, p. 162.
26. Petrov, *Soviet Gold* (New York, 1949), pp. 230–31.
27. Nicolaevsky, p. 53.
28. Orlov, p. 22; Walter Krivitsky, *I Was Stalin's Agent* (London, 1940), p. 186.
29. Khrushchev, Secret Speech.
30. Antonov-Ovseenko, p. 101.
31. Yakir, pp. 92, 120.
32. *Trotskyite-Zinovievite Terrorist Centre,* pp. 161–62.
33. Antonov-Ovseenko, p. 101.

Chapter X. The Third Story

1. Nicolaevsky, p. 56.
2. *Trotskyite-Zinovievite Terrorist Centre,* p. 174.

3. Nicolaevsky, p. 56.
4. Orlov, pp. 73–89; Nicolaevsky, p. 46.
5. Orlov, p. 73.
6. *Trotskyite-Zinovievite Terrorist Centre*, pp. 13, 31, 33, 158.
7. Orlov, p. 131.
8. *Kaizo*, April 1939.
9. Orlov, pp. 131–32.
10. *Trotskyite-Zinovievite Terrorist Centre*, p. 20.
11. Ibid., p. 28.
12. Ibid., p. 37.
13. Ibid., pp. 33–34.
14. Ibid., p. 31.
15. Ibid., pp. 21, 22, 36, 41, 43.
16. Ibid., p. 47.
17. See Conquest, *The Great Terror*, Chapter 4.
18. *Trotskyite-Zinovievite Terrorist Centre*, p. 47.
19. Ibid., p. 48.
20. Ibid., p. 30.
21. Ibid., p. 31.
22. Ibid., pp. 31, 33, 151.
23. Ibid., p. 31.
24. Ibid., p. 32.
25. Ibid., p. 146.
26. Ibid., pp. 34, 49, 61–62.
27. Ibid., p. 176.
28. Ibid., p. 148.
29. Ibid., p. 176.
30. Ibid., pp. 67, 70.
31. Orlov, p. 92.
32. *Trotskyite-Zinovievite Terrorist Centre*, p. 111.
33. Ibid., p. 34.
34. Ibid., pp. 31–33.
35. *Socialdemocraten*, 1 September 1936.
36. *Trotskyite-Zinovievite Terrorist Centre*, p. 67.
37. Ibid., p. 37.
38. Ibid., p. 33.
39. Ibid., p. 31.
40. *Bol'shaya sovetskaya entsiklopediya*, 3rd Ed.
41. Medvedev, p. 273.
42. *Belarusskaya savetskaya entsyklapedyya*.

43. Nicolaevsky, p. 64; Krivitsky, p. 207; Orlov, p. 209.
44. Orlov, pp. 131–32.

Chapter XI. The Fate of the Kirovites

1. *Literaturnaya gazeta,* 19 August 1987.
2. *Pravda,* 7 August 1936; *Oyonek,* No. 27, 1988.
3. *Leningradskaya pravda,* 6 July 1936.
4. Zavalishin MS.
5. *Latvijas padomju enciklopedija; Latvijas PSR maza enciklopedija.*
6. Zavalishin MS.
7. Antonov-Ovseenko, *Portret tirana,* p. 204.
8. *Pravda,* 2 December 1936.
9. *Pravda,* 31 October 1961.
10. *Pravda,* 4 December 1934.
11. Krasnikov, p. 188.
12. Khrushchev, Secret Speech.
13. *Nash Mironich,* p. 460.
14. Khrushchev, Secret Speech.
15. *Bolshaya sovetskaya entsiklopediya,* 3rd Ed.
16. *Latyshskaya sovetskaya entsyklopediya.* 1st and 2nd Eds.
17. Antonov-Ovseenko, pp. 94–95.
18. Medvedev, p. 237; Zavalishin MS.
19. *S. M. Kirov,* 3 Vols. (Moscow, 1935–1937).
20. *Zarya vostoka,* 17 February 1938.
21. Medvedev, p. 269.
22. *Bolshaya sovetskaya entsiklopediya,* 3rd Ed.
23. Mikhail S. Bernstam, "Yezhovshchina," Unpublished manuscript.
24. Krasnikov, p. 151.
25. Krasnikov, pp. 181–83; *Ocherki istorii Leningrada,* 4:383.
26. *Pravda,* 31 October 1961.
27. Antonov-Ovseenko, p. 211.
28. *Ocherki istorii Leningrada,* 4:383.
29. Zavalishin MS.
30. Ibid.
31. *Ocherki istorii Leningrada,* 4:383.
32. Ibid.
33. Zavalishin MS.
34. *Pravda,* 31 October 1961.

35. Yu. I. Zaretsky, "Neogubaemyi bol'shevik-leninets narodnyi tribun (k 100-letiu so dnia rozhdeniia S. M. Kirova)" *Voprosy istorii KPSS*, No. 3, 1986.

36. *Komsomolskaya pravda*, 15 January 1988.

Chapter XII. The Fourth Story

1. *Report of the Court Proceedings in the Case of the Anti-Soviet Trotskyite Centre* (Moscow, 1937), p. 89.

2. Ibid., p. 90.

3. Ibid., p. 94.

4. Ibid., p. 96.

5. Ibid.

6. Ibid., p. 72.

7. Ibid., p. 100.

8. Ibid., p. 543.

9. *Bloc of Rights and Trotskyites*, p. 771.

10. Ibid., p. 22.

11. *Pravda*, 20 December 1937.

12. Petrov, p. 172, 256.

13. *Bloc of Rights and Trotskyites*, pp. 22–28.

14. Ibid., pp. 29–34.

15. Orlov, p. 254.

16. *Bloc of Rights and Trotskyites*, p. 572.

17. Ibid., p. 681.

18. Ibid., p. 572.

19. Ibid., p. 376.

20. Ibid., p. 572.

21. Ibid., p. 678.

22. Ibid., p. 558.

23. Ibid., p. 376.

24. Ibid., p. 559.

25. Ibid., pp. 558–59.

26. Ibid., p. 35.

27. Ibid., p. 558.

28. Ibid., 796–97.

29. Ibid., p. 786.

30. Webbs, p. 1156.

31. *Bloc of Rights and Trotskyites*, p. 678.

Chapter XIII. Truths Emerge

1. *Byuleten oppozitsii*, No. 42, 1935.
2. L. Sedov, *Livre rouge sur le procès de Moscou* (Paris, 1936), p. 25.
3. Medevdev, *Bukharin*, pp. 116, 119.
4. Krivitsky, p. 186.
5. *New Leader*, 23 August 1941.
6. Barmine, pp. 252–53.
7. Gustav Herling, *A World Apart* (New York, 1951), p. 123.
8. Petrov, *Soviet Gold*, pp. 230–31.
9. Khrushchev, *Khrushchev Remembers*, p. 46.
10. Ibid., p. 61.
11. Orlov, pp. 28–29.
12. *Survey*, No. 50, January 1964, p. 143.
13. Teresa Toranska, *Them* (New York, 1987), p. 170.
14. Medvedev, p. 160; Antonov-Ovseenko, pp. 102ff.
15. Antonov-Ovseenko, p. 103.
16. Medvedev, p. 160.
17. Antonov-Ovseenko, p. 104.
18. *Pravda*, 19 May 1963.
19. *All-Union Conference on Measures to Improve the Training of Scientific-Pedagogical Cadres in the Historical Sciences* (Moscow, 1964), p. 298.
20. *Pravda*, 7 February 1964.
21. *Pravda*, 17 November 1961.
22. A. Solzhenitsyn, *The Oak and the Calf* (New York, 1980), p. 43.
23. Svetlana Alliluyeva, *Twenty Letters to a Friend* (London, 1967), p. 167.
24. Medvedev, pp. 159–61.
25. Antonov-Ovseenko, p. 91.
26. Anatoly Rybakov, "Deti Arbata," *Druzhba narodov*, No. 4–6, 1987; *Literaturnaya gazeta*, 19 August 1987.
27. *Yunost'* (Yaroslavl), 1 September 1987.
28. *Ogonek*, No. 50, 1987.

Chapter XIV. Verdict

1. *Trotskyite-Zinovievite Terrorist Centre*, pp. 31, 33.
2. Medvedev, p. 367.

3. Svetlana Alliluyeva, *Only One Year* (London, 1969), p. 190; Khrushchev, *Khrushchev Remembers,* pp. 261–62; *Sovetskaya Byelorussia* 13 January 1963.

4. See Conquest, *The Great Terror,* Chapter 6.

5. *Komsomolskaya pravda,* 2 April 1988.

6. Adam Ulam, *Stalin* (New York, 1972), pp. 385–87.

7. J. Arch Getty, *Origins of the Great Purges* (London, 1985), pp. 207–10.

8. *Yunost'* (Moscow), No. 3, 1988, p. 58.

9. Medvedev, p. 187.

10. Orlov, pp. 28–29.

11. Medvedev, p. 158; *Bloc of Rights and Trotskyites,* p. 796.

12. *Novoe russkoye slovo,* 20 June 1982.

13. Nicolaevsky, p. 101.

14. *Yunost'* (Yaroslavl), 1 September 1987.

15. *Sovetskaya Rossiya,* 23 August 1987, *Literaturnaya gazeta,* 23 December 1987.

16. *Proryv* (Moscow, 1988), p. 344.

17. *Russkaia mysl',* 29 May 1987.

18. *Yunost'* (Moscow), No. 3, 1988, p. 58.

19. *Moscow News,* No. 50, 1987.

20. *New York Times,* 16 January 1988.

21. *Le Monde,* 7–8 February 1988.

22. *Nedelya,* No. 7, 1988; *Baltimore Sun,* 26 February 1988.

23. *Daily Telegraph,* 7 November 1987.

24. *Trotskyite-Zinovievite Terrorist Centre,* pp. 135–38.

25. *Anti-Soviet Trotskyite Centre,* p. 487.

26. *Nedelya,* 1–7 February 1988.

Bibliography

Alexander Kosarev, Moscow, 1963.

Alliluyeva, Svetlana. *Only One Year.* London, 1969.

————. *Twenty Letters to a Friend.* London, 1967.

All-Union Conference on Measures to Improve the Training of Scientific-Pedagogical Cadres in the Historical Sciences, Moscow, 1964.

Antonov-Ovseenko, Anton. *Portret tirana.* New York, 1980.

————. *The Time of Stalin.* New York, 1981.

Astrakhanskiy front grazhdanskoy voine i S. M. Kirov. Stalingrad, 1937.

Barmine, Alexander. *One Who Survived.* New York, 1945.

Berger, Joseph. *Shipwreck of a Generation.* London, 1971.

Bernstam, Mikhail, "Yezhovshchina." Unpublished manuscript.

Benvenuti, F. "Kirov nella Politica Sovietica." *Annali dell'Instituto per gli Studi Storici* 4 (1973–1975).

Belarusskaya savetskaya entsyklapedyya.

Bol'shaia sovetskaya entsyklopediya, 3rd Edition.

Byuleten oppozitsii.

Ciliga, Anton. *The Russian Enigma.* London, 1940.

Cohen, Stephen F. *Bukharin and the Bolshevik Revolution.* New York, 1973.

Conquest, Robert. *The Great Terror.* New York, 1973.

————. *The Harvest of Sorrow.* New York, 1986.

The Crime of the Zinoviev Opposition. Moscow–Leningrad, 1935.

Deutscher, Isaac. *Stalin: A Political Biography.* London, 1949.

Dolunts, A. K. *Kirov na Severnom Kavkaze.* Moscow, 1973.

Dubinsky-Rukhadze, I. *Ordzhonikidze.* Moscow, 1963.

Getty, J. Arch. *Origins of the Great Purges.* London, 1985.

Ginzburg, Evgenia. *Journey into the Whirlwind.* New York, 1967.

Haslam, Jonathan. *Soviet Foreign Policy.* London, 1983.

————. *The Soviet Union and the Struggle for Collective Security in Europe.* London, 1984.

Henderson, Loy W. *A Question of Trust.* Stanford, 1980.

Herling, Gustav. *A World Apart.* New York, 1951.

Istoricheskiy arkhiv. No. 5, 1961.

Istoriia KPSS. 2nd Edition. Moscow, 1962.

Izvestiya.

Kaizo (Tokyo). April 1939.

Khrushchev, N. S. *Khrushchev Remembers.* New York, 1970.

————. Secret Speech to the XX Party Congress, 1956.

————. Speech to the XXII Party Congress, 1961.

Kirov, S. M. *Izbranniye statii i rechi* Moscow, 1957.

Komsomolskaya Pravda.

Kostiuk, Hrihory. *Stalinist Rule in the Ukraine.* Munich, 1960.

Kratkaya literaturnaya entsiklopedia. 2nd Edition.

Krasnikov, S. *Sergey Mironovich Kirov.* Moscow, 1964.

Kravchenko, Victor. *I Chose Justice.* London, 1951.

Krivitsky, Walter. *I Was Stalin's Agent.* London, 1940.

Latvijas padomju enciklopedija.

Latvijas PSR maza enciklopedija.

Lenin, V. I. *Polnoe sobranie sochinenii.* 5th Edition. Moscow, 1965–1975.

Lermolo, Elizabeth. *Face of a Victim.* London, 1956.

Leningradskaya pravda.

Literaturnaya gazeta.

Medvedev, Roy. *Let History Judge.* New York, 1971.

————. *On Stalin and Stalinism.* Oxford, 1979.

————. *Nikolai Bukharin.* New York, 1980.

Nash Mironich. Leningrad, 1969.

Nedelya (Moscow).

New Leader (New York).

Nicolaevsky Archive, Hoover Institution Archives, Series 178.

Nicolaevsky, Boris. *Power and the Soviet Elite.* New York, 1965.

Novoe Russkoye Slovo.

Ocherki istorii kommunisticheskoi partii Gruzii. Tblisi, 1971.

Ocherki istorii Leningrada. Moscow-Leningrad, 1964.

Ogonek.

Orlov, Alexander. *The Secret History of Stalin's Crimes.* London, 1954.

Petrov, V. *It Happens in Russia.* London, 1951.

———. *Soviet Gold.* New York, 1949.

Pidhainy, S., ed. *The Black Deeds of the Kremlin.* Vol. 1., Toronto, 1953.

Pravda.

Proceedings of the VII Congress of the Komsomol. Moscow, 1926.

Proryv. Moscow, 1988.

Report of the Court Proceedings: The Case of the Trotskyite-Zinovievite Terrorist Centre. English Edition. Moscow, 1936.

Report of the Court Proceedings in the Case of the Anti-Soviet "Bloc of Rights and Trotskyites." English Edition. Moscow, 1938.

Report of the Court Proceedings in the Case of the Anti-Soviet Trotskyite Centre. Moscow, 1937.

Rybakov, Anatoly. "Deti Arbata." *Druzhba narodov,* No. 4–6, 1987.

S. M. Kirov. 3 Vols. Moscow, 1935–1937.

S. M. Kirov v Leningrade. Leningrad, 1966.

Sedov, L. *Livre rouge sur le procès de Moscou.* Paris, 1936.

Shatunovskaya, Lidiya. *Zhizn' v kremle.* New York, 1982.

Silin, P. "Astrakhanskie rastrely," in *Cheka.* Berlin, 1922.

Sinelnikov, S. M. *Kirov.* Moscow, 1964.

———. *Sto stranits o Sergee Kirove.* Leningrad, 1968.

Solzhenitsyn, Aleksandr. *The Oak and the Calf.* New York, 1980.

Sotsialisticheskii vestnik.

Sovetskaya byelorussia.

Sovetskaya molodezh.

Stenographic Report of the XVII Party Congress.

Survey. No. 50, January 1964.

Stalin, I. V. *Sochineniia.* Moscow, 1946–1955.

Toranska, Teresa. *Them.* New York, 1987.

Trotsky, Leon. *La bureaucratie stalinienne et l'assassinat de Kirov.* Paris, c. 1935.

Ulam, Adam. *Stalin.* New York, 1972.

United Kingdom, Foreign Office, F. O. 371, N1868:6.35.

Vestnik Leningradskogo Universiteta. No. 8, 1968.

Voprosy istorii kommunisticheskoi partii Kazakhstana. Alma-Ata, 1968.

Vremya i my. No. 70. 1983.

Webb, Sidney and Beatrice. *Soviet Communism: A New Civilization.* 2nd Ed. London, 1937.

Who Was Who in the USSR. Metuchen, N.J., 1972.

Yakir, Peter. *A Childhood in Prison.* London, 1973.

Yunost' (Moscow).

Yunost' (Yaroslavl).

Zaretsky, Yu. I. "Neogubaemyi bol'shevik-leninets narodnyi tribun (k 100-letiu so dnia rozhdeniia S. M. Kirova)" *Voprosy istorii KPSS.* No. 3, 1986.

Zarya vostoka.

Zavalishin, V. K. Manuscript in Nicolaevsky Archive, Hoover Institution Archives.

Index

161